RON CRAYCRAFT

LIVING IN THE SUPERNATURAL

God's Way to Absolute Victory

The *"storms of life"* will threaten to
"rock your world."
But your *personal forecast* of God's Word will bring hope,
healing, faith, love, peace and victory
through Christ Jesus.

Ron Craycraft
Senior Pastor, Forecast For Life Church

CONTENTS

PSALM 91:1-2

He who dwells in the secret place of the Most High Shall abide under the shadow of the Almighty.

[2]I will say of the Lord, "He is my refuge and my fortress; My God, in Him I will trust."

Chapter 1

FINDING A SAFE PLACE

A ll of a sudden, the car that had just passed by wheeled around with screeching tires in a furious u-turn. There were fists hanging out the window and shouts of threatening profanity, "You're dead-meat now – you punks!"

There were four of us boys walking home from school. This out-of-control car was obviously headed straight for us! Apparently, these older teens thought we were throwing rocks at their car. Uh-oh!

We were always throwing rocks as we walked home, you know, just off into the fields or at signs or at just "nothing." It was obvious that these older boys were not getting ready for just an argument about what direction our rocks were going. Surely, I would never throw at cars! (I don't know about my friend Sammy.)

Finding a Safe Place

We took off running. George and Walter zoomed off in one direc- tion. I followed Sammy in another direction. If only we could find a place to hide, we were both thinking the same thing – frantically!

It seemed as though Sammy had a plan as I followed him running as fast as I could. I don't know if Sammy grew tired or if he was just ready to give in and take his beating – but he ran into a small area between two houses. I followed.

It was not a good plan. It was not a safe hiding place at all. We cowered in this small, confined area for less than a minute, and two of the older boys found us. Fortunately, one of the boys was Sammy's neighbor – so they just pushed us around a little bit and let us go. Whew!

George and Walter were not so fortunate, but I will spare you the details.

The point is that we all face danger on a daily basis and many times wish that somehow we could find a place of protection and safety.

A Real Place of Safety

There "is" a special place that can give you super-natural peace, power, provision and protection during the "storms of life" — when your mind goes blank and your body is weak and sickly. This special place is in the supernatural, unseen world. In order to understand this place, you'll have to begin by admitting that you don't know everything. You'll have to be a born again, Spirit-led believer. You'll have to believe that there is no real truth that does not agree with the Word of God. The Holy Spirit, His gifts, and supernatural living will always agree with the Holy Bible.

Living supernaturally is not complicated, weird, religious, or spooky. I realize that you have probably met someone who talked about the supernatural – but they acted so religious and weird that you weren't at all attracted to them. Make no mistake, living supernaturally is God's will for you. It's the only safe way to live with an abundance of peace, joy, divine health and real prosperity.

You can live supernaturally when you have first-hand knowledge of God's secret place. You'll soon find out that you can be "in the secret place" wherever you are — at work, driving, in prison, in school, in the hospital, or on vacation.

Paul was in the secret place when he was in prison with Silas. Stephen was in the secret place just before they stoned his body. Peter was in the secret place when he was in a trance, praying. Paul was in the secret place when he was carried up to the third Heaven.

The secret place is the place where God's covenant promises of protection and provision are made available to us!

He who dwells in the secret place of the Most High
Shall abide under the shadow of the Almighty.

Psalm 91

Supernatural Power Or Foolishness

"Oh no – not again!" Behind me I heard screeching tires – again! A car was pulled off to the side of the road and out jumps an older boy, running straight toward me! This could not be happening again! (It was only a few days since the last mistaken incident about rock throwing.)

I took off running. This time I decided to zip across this empty parking lot. Oops! Within two or three steps, I knew the chase was over. It was a totally enclosed, private parking lot to an apartment complex. I was trapped.

The next thing I felt was a one-two punch to the face. It seemed like time was in slow motion. It seemed that I had time to think over several options. My first thought was remembering that there was no place to hide at all. The second thought was that I would have to begin fighting back. My face was already numb; so I might as well go down swinging!

The point is that many people think there are no options in life except to go down swinging. But if we look to the Creator of the universe, no circumstance is too hopeless for His supernatural power.

In God's secret place, there is safety, protection, and deliverance from trouble.

The sad thing is that many Christians have not been taught about the secret place. Still other Christians will not be bold enough to "live" in the secret place.

The Secret Is Revealed

The secret place that is described in Psalm 91 is a place provided by the Lord God to give us real life protection, healing, and deliverance from trouble. Any believer could always meditate, pray and speak God's Word and receive the benefits of God's secret place. When you abide in God's Word and abide in God's secret place, you'll be in God's presence!

The fullness of God's secret place was and is now revealed "In Christ Jesus!"

Now fasten your spiritual seatbelt! The Father God is in the "secret place!" Jesus said, "I am in the Father and the Father is in Me." (John 10:38; John 14:11; Matthew 6:6.) The Father God has given us great and precious promises of love, protection, and provision with His blood covenant oath – established with the blood of Jesus at the Cross.

We Need Revelation Knowledge of God's Covenant

The basis of all the promises of God – which includes protection, favor, spiritual power, healing, and salvation is the blood of God's covenant. Understanding the blood covenant will strengthen your faith in a way that I believe few revelations from God's Word will do for you. Unfortunately, the western branch of the body of Christ is totally ignorant of the blood covenant.

They are like the description Paul gives in Ephesians 2:12: "Remember that at that time you were separate from Christ, excluded from citizenship in Israel and *foreigners to the covenants of the promise*, without hope and without God in the world."

The concept of covenant is "*foreign*" to many believers. The reason is because they have been far removed from seeing covenants practiced in everyday life. They have witnessed "contracts" instead of "covenants."

A covenant is a contract, but it is ratified in blood and the agreement is all-inclusive—everything that belongs to one party belongs to the other party as well.

In a contract you may purchase a car and in exchange you give a certain amount of money to the company, and in trade they give you use of the car. You don't own the company and they don't own you. But in a covenant, you own everything the covenant party owns and they own everything you own; you take all their assets and liabilities and they do likewise.

Jesus made a covenant with us, not a simple contract. At the Passover, Jesus took bread and wine and lifted it up and said, "This is blood of the covenant" (Matt 26:28). He did not sit down at a table and sign with ink an agreement.

A blood covenant binds the parties together, so they are not free to do "anything" they wish; they must fulfill the obligations of the blood covenant. This is the only basis that we can have faith in God. Without the wonderful covenant promises of God, there would be no solid foundation for our faith. We could not be sure what God's will was if He had not bound Himself to a blood oath. (Hebrews 6:17-19.) With this solid faith in God, we are ready to tap into the supernatural life that God has had planned for us since the beginning.

Qualified by Christ

We are all qualified to live a supernatural life because of the blood of Jesus. And not just to rise above silly little circumstances like I just shared with you about needing a hiding place. We are called by Jesus to live an "abundant life." (John 10:10.) We're qualified to speak with new tongues, cast out demons, lay hands on the sick to recover, and copy the works Jesus did. (Matthew 16:17-18.)

If you're a believer, you are called to live a supernatural life. You're qualified to be empowered in every area—spirit, soul, body, finances, relationships, and everything else that pertains to life and godliness.

You might be thinking, "Those are wonderful and encouraging words – but how do I get that to happen in my life?

There's only one way to live a supernatural life — "know" Christ, hear His voice, and be an imitator of the Lord Jesus. If we want the life Jesus came to earth to give us, then we must do the things Jesus did – to get the results that Jesus had.

Chapter 2

WALKING IN THE SPIRIT

I heard the story of a woman who was mugged in the downtown district of her city. She was calling a prayer line, and very upset. She told how she was hit in the head and knocked down while the thief ran away with her purse.

"The reason that I'm calling in for prayer," she related, is not really because I'm hurt. It's because I'm confused and my faith is shaken."

"How so," replied the prayer minister.

"You see, I pray for, believe, and receive the Lords' protection every morning – declaring and confessing the 91st Psalm.

The prayer minister paused for a few minutes – then began to ask about her trip downtown. "Did you have important business in the downtown area?" "Not really," she answered. "Did you have a check in your spirit about not going to a dangerous area?"

"Yes I did, but I figured that by standing on God's promises, I would be protected anyway."

This is a perfect example of how we should always live with Holy Spirit power AND the Word of God. The Holy Spirit and the Word of God always work together – they are "One" and always agree!

> *"For as many as are led by the Spirit of God, these are sons of God."*
>
> Romans 8:14

It's a Matter of Life and Death

Life is full of twists and turns, and we are constantly faced with decisions that can either move us further into the will of God for our lives or farther away from it.

In these last days, it's going to be imperative that we be able to hear God's voice and follow the leading of the Holy Spirit every step of the way. In fact, I will go so far as to say that your very life could depend on it. Walking in the Spirit is the way God designed us to live as Believers. We possess recreated spirits that are infused with the life and wisdom of God. The Holy Spirit resides in our born again spirits, and when we renew our minds with the Word, we can begin to receive "downloaded" information from heaven that can lead us into a life of abundance, prosperity, protection, and peace.

The Word of God instructs us to "walk in the Spirit" in Galatians 5:16. What does it mean to walk in the Spirit? Walking in the Spirit is twofold. First, it means to walk according to the Word of God. Jesus said in John 6:63, "*It is the spirit that quickeneth; the flesh profiteth nothing: the words that I speak unto you, they are spirit, and they are life.*" Jesus' words are spiritual because He *is* the Word of God. Therefore, when we walk according to the Word of God, we are walking "in the Spirit." So we know that walking in the Spirit means walking according to the written Word of God.

The second aspect of walking in the Spirit is related to following the leadership of the Holy Spirit. The Holy Spirit is our teacher, and the Word says that He will lead and guide us into all truth (John 16:13). The Holy Spirit only speaks what He hears the Father say, so when you become tuned into His voice and direction, you can be confident that you are going in the right direction. Living a Spirit-led life, every moment of every day, is the other component of walking in the Spirit. It is the fail-proof way to achieve victory and success in your day-to-day life.

Sharpen Your Spiritual Ears

Walking in the Spirit is not something the Lord casually asks us to do; we are charged to do it. We are not supposed to be led by our flesh, our unrenewed soul, or any other voice besides the voice of God's Word. Many people cannot distinguish the voice of the Holy Spirit and, consequently, they are not able to be led by Him. Recognizing the Holy Spirit's voice comes from spending time in the Word. His voice will always be in agreement with what is written in the Bible. God's methods of operation have not changed, which is why the Holy Spirit is never going to tell you to do something that violates the written Word of God.

Another way to sharpen your spiritual ears is to pray in the Spirit, or pray in tongues. Praying in tongues allows you to pray to God, spirit to Spirit. When you pray in your heavenly language, you are bypassing your soul (mind, will, and emotions) and communicating on the purest spiritual level possible. Praying in tongues makes your spirit more sensitive and allows you to tap into direct revelation from heaven. The Holy Spirit prays through you when you pray in tongues, interceding for people and situations you don't even know about. This is a direct line of communication to the spiritual realm that always gets results.

Walking in the Spirit takes a commitment to choose God's way of doing things over the way of the flesh. In fact, when we walk in the Spirit, we will not fulfill the lusts of the flesh. It is God's formula for overcoming the temptations and attacks of the enemy. Keeping ourselves immersed in the Word and praying frequently in the Holy Spirit are the sure-fire ways to maintain a Spirit-led existence.

Regardless of your level of spiritual development, you can always go to higher heights, and deeper depths in God. You can determine the intensity and acceleration of your growth by your commitment to God's Word and your commitment to prayer. Walking in the Spirit liberates you from the desires of the carnal mind, and frees you to live a supernatural existence that's in a constant state of going from glory to glory. Your life will never be the same!

In His Presence

Do you sometimes believe that you can accomplish more on your own, without any help from God? Do you often start your day without even acknowledging His presence? If so, I want to challenge you to begin seeking Him—not just in the morning—but throughout your day. Personally, I take advantage of every opportunity I can to find a quiet place where I can be alone to talk with God, just as I would a close friend. When we cultivate a personal relationship with God, we learn that His way is always better than our own.

Often it seems as if the methods of the world are quicker and easier than God's method; however, I know from experience that His way is always best. Following the world leads to a dead end. However, following God's way leads to a successful, happy life.

Many times, we rush through our days, proceed with our own plans, and place our time with God on the backburner. As a result, we often travel down those dead-end roads. Only when everything else has failed do we call out to him in desperation. Although God doesn't mind showing us mercy during those times, He would rather we seek Him first. Just as a close friend would not want to be chosen as a last resort, God doesn't want to be our last resort either.

When we cultivate a relationship with God, we must understand that He not only wants to be an intricate part of our lives, but He also wants us to delight in the time we spend with Him. When we begin to enjoy spending time with Him, He allows us to know Him on a more intimate level. He reveals mysteries to us when we quiet ourselves and listen more intently for His voice. He will give us answers that only He can give, which will empower us to reach our fullest potential in life.

As we receive His words, we experience a peace that passes all understanding. We begin to have what I call a knowing, deep inside, that He is always there, ready to give us the revelation knowledge we need to operate in power.

In order to reach this secret place, we must keep in mind certain truths that are vital in establishing a relationship with Him. First, we must acknowledge His son, Jesus, who sacrificed His precious blood. I can't emphasize enough the importance of acknowledging the shed blood of Jesus. It is a necessity in the life of a Believer. It is only because of Jesus' sacrifice that we have an opportunity to cultivate a close relationship with the Father.

Also, we must love others unconditionally, because God is love. When we begin to increase our understanding of the love of God and operate in it, we will begin to experience more of Him.

Last but not least, we must learn how to cast our cares on Him, setting aside time each day to clear our minds of clutter. God is always speaking to us, but when our minds are filled with worries and concerns we cannot hear Him!

The answers to the problems you have been struggling with are waiting for you in His presence. I encourage you to begin to seek Him today. Take your relationship with the Lord to a deeper level by giving Him the opportunity to speak into your life—then quickly obey what you hear. Make spending time with Him your new daily habit. And I am confident that you will be so glad you did.

The Voice Behind the Word

Although God has promised victory for every Believer, it is not uncommon to experience moments when our faith is under attack. During these times, we tend to wonder if we will ever receive real answers to our prayers, and we may ask ourselves, *how can I tap into the hidden wisdom of God that will bring forth my breakthrough?* The key is hearing God's voice behind His written Word.

To identify God's voice, we must actively communicate with Him. If we want to hear from Him, we must fellowship with Him through regular meditation on His Word and consistent prayer. As Believers who have been filled with the Holy Spirit, we can also speak to God by praying in tongues. Through praying in the Spirit, we speak the very mysteries that could unlock the answers to the situations we face in life!

Speaking in tongues is not just babbling. It is an intimate form of communication with God. First Corinthians 2:7 says, *"But we speak the wisdom of God in a mystery, even the hidden wisdom, which God ordained before the world unto our glory...."* According to 1 Corinthians 14:2, when you speak in tongues, you are speaking directly to God in a Heavenly language! Each time you pray in the spirit, hidden wisdom is revealed, and you allow the Holy Spirit to show you things that are hidden from everyone else—even the devil.

There is something powerful that happens when we spend time praying in tongues. It is often during the quiet times that follow that we hear the voice of God speaking truth and wisdom directly from

Heaven. You may be driving your car or ironing your clothes one day, for example, and the Holy Spirit will give you the revelation you need during those intimate moments with the Lord.

You will experience great success in your life when you clearly hear the voice of God. Most people can read the Bible and gain some understanding of it, but when you are able to hear God's voice behind a scripture or sermon and allow the Holy Spirit to show you how it applies to your specific situation, you will experience real breakthrough.

Through God we have access to wealth, healing, deliverance, peace, and so much more. He wants to speak to you about any situation you are facing in life. When you spend time with Him in prayer and in His Word, you open the door for Him to speak a word that will help you. Listen to the voice of God behind Scriptures for maximum results!

When you learn to hear God's voice, He will give you the insight you need to strengthen your relationship with Him. Be sure to visit our online bookstore today and discover a myriad of products and resources that will help you grow spiritually.

Two Realms, One Reality

In these last days before Jesus returns, people are searching for answers; they want to know about life, death, and what happens beyond the grave. I would go so far as to say the majority of people, deep down, are even frightened about this whole topic. As a result, personal opinions are formed and "logical" conclusions are reached, based on what makes sense to the intellect and what feels comfortable. However, understanding spiritual things can only take place when we move beyond our own opinions, and what we can understand with our natural minds.

Spiritual realities are just as real as the tangible things we perceive with our five senses. There is more to life than what meets the eye; the natural eye that is. There are two realms running concurrently—the spiritual realm, and the physical realm. Both realms are as real as the other. In fact, the spiritual realm is even more real because it is what I like to call the "parent realm." In other words, everything originates there. What we perceive with our five senses changes and pass away, but spiritual realities are eternal, meaning they will exist forever. This is what makes the spiritual realm superior to the natural.

Now, whether or not you believe in a spiritual realm does not negate the truth that it indeed exists! It contains spiritual matter, beings, and activities that affect what goes on in the Earth. In the realm of the spirit, there are forces of good and evil, God and Satan, angels and demons. This may sound like something out of a science fiction movie but it is no fairy tale. It is real and taking place right now. There are two kingdoms in operation: the Kingdom of God and the Kingdom of Darkness. In the first, Jesus Christ is Lord; the second is headed by Satan and his forces. The battle that rages on a constant basis is for the souls of men.

I know there are those who may ask, How do you know these things are real? How do you know there is more to life than what I can see? I like to use the illustration of electricity. You cannot see the electrical currents that produce light and heat, but you can experience the results of electricity. When you flip a light switch, the lights come on, and when you turn on a gas stove, a flame emerges. What you cannot see produces something in the natural realm that you can see. The same is true with the spirit realm; even though you cannot see the spiritual activity taking place with your eyes, you will eventually see the results of that activity in the Earth.

The questions are, who, and what do you believe? Believing these truths is a matter of faith. Just like electricity, you believe it exists even though you cannot see it. Faith is the main ingredient that allows us to access the reality that there are unseen forces at work, beyond what we can perceive with our senses. At some point we all have to come to a place of believing God or not. We simply cannot go beyond what we believe to be true.

We need to consider the truth of the spiritual realm from the Word of God, in order to build our faith that it does indeed exist. As you come on this journey, ask the Holy Spirit to illuminate the words you read and open your eyes to these things. Ask Him to give you understanding about the realm of the spirit. He doesn't leave anyone in the dark about what is and what is to come. Even if you have never heard this information before, open yourself to the possibility of its truth.

You've Already Got It!

When you accepted Jesus Christ as your personal Lord and Savior, the Holy Spirit moved in and became one with your spirit (Ephesians 1:13). Everything about the Holy Spirit is now true about you, because you're one with Him.

Ephesians 3:16 says the Holy Spirit, Who now resides in you, released the spirit of might—the ability to do all things—on the inside of you. Ephesians 1:19, 20 says the very power that raised Jesus from the dead—that immeasurable, unlimited power—has been put on the inside of you. Zoë life has been put on the inside of you. Then, 1 John 4:17 says, *"As he is, so are we in this world."*

That's a powerful thing. Right now, you who are born again possess God's "might." I know it's hard for some of you to grasp that truth, because the Bible refers to God as the *Almighty God.* So how can we, mere humans, be as mighty as God?

Might is the ability to do all things. We've already established that the Holy Spirit has released the Spirit of might on the inside of you. It's in there!

Now, in the Old Testament, the Spirit of might was not on the inside of people; it had to *come* on them. Take Elijah, for example. The Bible says the hand of God came mightily upon him, and he outran Ahab's chariots to the entrance of Jezreel. (1 Kings 18:46.)

It's important that we discern Old Testament truth from New Testament truth. People in the Old Testament were not born again. Their spirits had not been recreated. They didn't have this injection of power, in the person of the Holy Spirit, on the inside. Study it out for yourself (1 Samuel 5:6; 2 Kings 3:15; Ezra 7:6, 28; Ezekiel 3:14). The hand of God, His might, *came* upon all of those Old Testament prophets. But today, it's in us. It's eternally residing in us.

You may be thinking, "But, I didn't deserve it." That's my point. It's in you by grace! If you live for one hundred years, you couldn't earn or deserve it. The Bible says you're saved by grace through faith (Ephesians 2:8). Salvation is a free gift from God. So is grace (Romans 5:15).

You're walking around with every answer to every prayer. Some of you are struggling financially, and you don't even know you've got millionaire potential inside you. You're sick, and healing power is inside you. You're not happy, and the joy of the Lord is inside you. But you're satisfied with acting like a mere human, continuing to ignore this grace that richly abounds toward you! (2 Corinthians 9:8).

The key to withdrawing from your spirit, from the supernatural realm, is to renew your mind with the Word of God. All of your old thought patterns come from the world. If you don't renew your mind with the Word, you're only going to believe what you've believed all of your life, before you got saved. You will only believe what you can sense with your five physical senses.

Mind renewal takes time; it's a daily process. It's an exchange process. You have to begin to allow God's Word to change the way you think. It starts with reading the Bible on a daily basis so you'll know how to adjust your thinking. You exchange your old thoughts for the Word of God thoughts. You renew your mind so it agrees with your new, born-again spirit.

If you want results, you can't ignore this process. As you renew your mind, you'll begin to see great, significant change in your life. You'll pull proof over into the natural realm from the supernatural realm, and prove the good, acceptable, and perfect will of God for your life!

> *"Don't copy the behavior and customs of this world, but let God transform you into a new person by changing the way you think. Then you will learn to know God's will for you, which is good and pleasing and perfect."*
>
> Romans 12:2, *NLT*

If you're born again, you are God's own workmanship, His own handiwork, *recreated* in Christ Jesus! (Ephesians 2:10). The Holy Spirit dwells in your born-again spirit, so it is perfect, flawless. It's just like God!

It's time to begin living the good life that God prearranged and made ready for you to live!

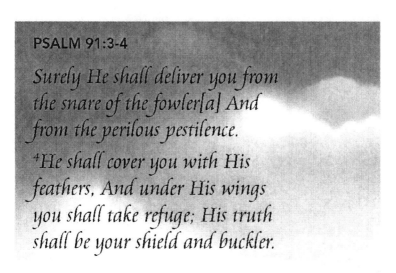

PSALM 91:3-4

Surely He shall deliver you from the snare of the fowler[a] And from the perilous pestilence.
⁴He shall cover you with His feathers, And under His wings you shall take refuge; His truth shall be your shield and buckler.

Chapter 3

SUPERNATURAL HELP FROM HEAVEN

I pray and sing "in the spirit" every day. I surrender my own will to the leading and teaching of the Holy Spirit—and begin to privately pray with a wonderful heavenly, unknown tongue.

Does that Surprise you?

No matter where we are on planet earth, we can enter the "secret place" of prayer to the Most High God—in the wonderful name of Jesus—where the Holy Spirit gives powerful holy sounds, syllables, and spiritual words. It's the true worship *"in the spirit."*—that our Lord Jesus taught about. (See John 4:23-24 and 1 Corinthians 14:14.)

It's the same phrase used by the apostles Paul and John. It's a private, supernatural prayer to the Heavenly Father, through the Holy Spirit, in Jesus' name.

Humbling ourselves "in the presence of the Lord" is one the most awesome things we can experience on planet earth!

Have We Resisted the Wrong Thing?

Don't misunderstand. At first I did not want this to happen to me. I was just like a lot of other Christians that are discouraged (by well-meaning church leaders) from receiving something thought to be un-natural and not normal.

When I heard the good news that the Holy Spirit is alive and well on planet earth, I was amazed and very hungry to find out more! You see living a normal, natural life is really just conforming to what society, organized religion, and the 6 O'clock News tells us.

Shouldn't we be living by what Heaven tells us?

It's sad to see that many well-meaning Christians are living the "same ole, same ole" life—waking up to another day of going to work, coming home, and watching TV—then praying for the weekend, to get some temporary desires satisfied.

What if life could be an exciting adventure every day?

What if we could live life in a super-natural way—doing the works of Jesus and helping people with words and healing from heaven?

We can! We can soar much higher than our physical senses can take us. *(Jesus promised that we could.)*

It's Better If I Go Away

The disciples of Jesus were "eye-witnesses" to the most phenomenal and glorious miracles the world has ever seen!

The disciples were amazed as blind eyes were opened and the dead were raised to life. The disciples heard Jesus command a raging storm to die and a fig tree to wither. They saw thousands fed as Jesus multiplied a few fish and loaves of bread. The words of many prophets of God were coming to pass right before their very eyes!

Never before had mankind witnessed the miraculous hand of God in such an overwhelming and personal way.

Yet, as wonderful as things seemed to be—the disciples were told by Jesus Himself that it would be better if He went away. He said that the Heavenly Father had a far more excellent plan for them—and it would be to their "advantage" if He returned to heaven. (See John 16.)

The Holy Spirit Is Waiting On You

You are not an accident. God has a divine plan for your life, and this great plan will be fulfilled as you are led by the power of the Holy Spirit!

The number one thing you and I need to know is that God cares about you. He loves you!

> *For I know the thoughts that I think toward you, says*
> *the LORD, thoughts of peace and not of evil, to give*
> *you a future and a hope. Then you will call upon Me*
> *and go and pray to Me, and I will listen to you. And*
> *you will seek Me and find Me, when you search for*
> *Me with all your heart.*
>
> Jeremiah 29:11-13

The second thing that we should all realize is that *"God is on our side,"* we do not have to fear the unseen, supernatural world if we trust our Creator. (See Psalm 118:6.)

The "Unseen" World Is Real

If we are going to trust in the Lord for a blessed life, then one vital fact should be settled in our thinking: The "unseen" world is more real than the seen world—and this supernatural world has a dramatic effect on everything that happens in the "seen" world.

In the unseen world there are angelic spirits and demonic spirits, there is a real heaven and a real hell—and of course there is the unseen Lord God Himself, Creator and Sustainer of everything!

Another thing to remember when you are praying to receive the "secret power of God, the Holy Spirit," is that He is a gentleman and will never force you—but always waits until you open your heart to choose Him.

Your spirit—your heart—the "hidden man of the heart"—the eternal you on the inside—has been made in the image of God.

You might be thinking: *"That doesn't sound like what I have heard in my church."*

You're right! Usually the only time we hear anything about the unseen world is at funerals. Do you want to wait until your funeral to find out if there is really an invisible world?

The Bible definition of faith is that it is the substance and evidence of things that cannot be seen.

"Everyone" Has Faith in The Unseen

Everyone has faith and everyone believes . . . something.

What about your actions when the weather predictions are indicating a major storm might be heading your way? You look outside and it's a clear day, yet you start making plans to take cover, relocate, or board everything up. By faith you start acting based on what you have been told.

Most of our everyday activities are done by faith.

Do you wake up every morning and head toward your car by faith, believing that it will start and get you to work? It is something that you cannot see while you are in the shower, but your evidence is that the mechanic said the vehicle is all tuned up and ready to go.

What do you do when your boss tells you that a firing is about to take place if you do not get to work? By faith you believe it and get back to work. Your evidence? The person that used to sit next to you until last week is not there anymore.

You can't see the air you breathe (I'm not talking about polluted air). But there is "unseen" evidence that air is flowing through your lungs and you are alive!

You can't see atomic or hydrogen molecules, but we believe that our world is in danger every day because of "nuclear" weapons. The evidence? We have been given detailed physical evidence by reputable news reporters, scientists, and historians.

Human beings were created to live by faith.

> *For since the creation of the world His invisible attributes are clearly seen, being understood by the things that are made, even His eternal power and Godhead, so that they are without excuse.*
>
> Romans 1:20

We Need Help from Heaven

It is imperative that we get an understanding that there is an unseen world all around us.

If you are searching for the safest way to live in this violent world, and are not satisfied with typical religious thinking, you have to know how to get help from Heaven.

Satan is active and deceiving and destroying on planet earth today. He makes himself visible by every evil manifestation that you can see. Look around.

The works of the devil are obvious in every corner of the world, in every news broadcast, in every mental institution, in every devil worshipping cult, and in every poverty stricken 3rd world country. However, I do not want to give "the salesman of fear" any more press. What we need is to magnify the goodness of Almighty God. God is love, He offers hope, supernatural protection, and gives real peace to overcome the evil of this seen and unseen world.

In light of the many examples in God's Word (Jesus, Noah, Abraham, David, Daniel, Joshua, Moses, Elijah, Peter, and Paul), we can expect supernatural protection. God's promises belong to us. It's not because of anything we have done. It's entirely because of what Jesus has done.

Are there conditions to God's protection? Absolutely.

Have we fulfilled all of the conditions? Not by a long shot.

We have a long way to go in order to get ourselves to believe what God has promised. But we can get there!

Believe Before You See

Remember the Lord's Prayer? *"Thy will be done on earth as it is in Heaven."* Jesus was calling for God's will, from the unseen heaven, to be done in the earth. In the book of James we are taught that, *"every good and perfect gift comes down from the Father of Lights,"* (James 1:17).

So, our prayers are calling for God's goodness in the "unseen" world of Heaven, to manifest in our "seen" world.

Having said that, we should also consider that human nature is to say; *"I'll believe it when I see it."*

But the truth is that we need to believe "first."

29

If there was ever a generation where people need to be aware of God's "unseen" world and know how things operate there, it's this generation.

You'll never understand the truth of God's Creation, His ways, His Word—unless you "submit" your own will and ways to God's Will and ways.

It's A "Hidden" Secret

The most wonderful promises of God are reserved especially for "you" – the born again, Spirit-filled believer!

> *"Attaining to all riches of the full assurance of understanding, to the knowledge of the mystery of God, both of the Father and of Christ, In whom are hidden all the treasures of wisdom and knowledge,"*
> Colossians 2:2b-3

It is the "unsearchable riches of Christ that "unbelievers" cannot understand. Our preaching of the Good News is to *"make all see what is the fellowship of the mystery, which from the beginning of the ages has been hidden in God who created all things through Jesus Christ,"* (Ephesians 3:9).

The wonderful mysteries of the goodness of God are hidden from the devil, enemies of the cross, and anyone who practices evil.

> *"But we speak the wisdom of God in a mystery, the hidden wisdom which God ordained before the ages for our glory. Which none of the rulers of this age knew; for had they known, they would not have crucified the Lord of glory"*
> 1 Corinthians 2:7-8

But as it is written:

"Eye has not seen, nor ear heard, Nor have entered into the heart of man the things which God has prepared for those who love Him."

"But God has revealed them to us through His Spirit. For the Spirit searches all things, yes, the deep things of God"

1 Corinthians 2:9-10

God's Will Is the Baptism With the Holy Spirit

You have been involved with the Holy Spirit since you first accepted Jesus as your Lord and Savior.

When you prayed a sincere prayer according to Romans 10:9 and confessed that Jesus was raised from the dead to give you salvation—it was the Holy Spirit who performed the miracle of the "new birth" of your spirit.

1st Corinthians 12:3 states that no one says *"Jesus is Lord"* except by the Holy Spirit.

Jesus Himself told the men who walked by His side for 3 years that it is to their "advantage" if He went away and sent them the Holy Spirit.

Just think of that!

Would you like the inside information that will guide you through the bad news and uncertainties of this world?

All you have to do is ask the Father in Jesus' name to be filled with the Holy Spirit. Your only job is to believe and receive—and Jesus has promised to baptize you with the overflowing "rivers of living water" power of the Holy Spirit!

"So I say to you, ask, and it will be given to you; seek, and you will find; knock, and it will be opened to you. For everyone who asks receives, and he who seeks finds, and to him who knocks it will be opened. If a son asks for bread from any father among you, will he give him a stone? Or if he asks for a fish, will he give him a serpent instead of a fish? Or if he

*asks for an egg, will he offer him a scorpion? If you
then, being evil, know how to give good gifts to your
children, how much more will your heavenly Father
give the Holy Spirit to those who ask Him!"*

Luke 11:9-13

The Power of the Holy Spirit In You

Believers today have vastly underestimated the power of the Holy Spirit.

You may wonder how I can be so sure of that. It's simple, really. If we truly understood and believed what the Bible tells us about Him, we would never worry about anything again. All hell has to offer could come against us and we wouldn't fear. We'd just grin and say, "I'm an overcomer and more than a conqueror! The Greater One lives within me and He has given me all the wisdom, strength, power and provision I need to rise above every storm." "Glory to God!"

Right now you may think you could never have that kind of boldness. But let me ask you something: What would you do if Jesus appeared to you today? How would you act if He linked His arm in yours and told you that from now on, He would be physically present with you in every situation? If you became sick, He would lay His hand on you and you'd be healed. If you ran short of money, He'd pray and multiply your resources. If you encountered a problem you didn't know how to handle, He'd tell you exactly what to do.

Under those circumstances, you'd be very bold and confident, wouldn't you? Every time you ran into trouble, you'd just glance over at Jesus standing next to you and suddenly, you'd have great courage.

Of course, there's one problem. The fact is, you don't have that advantage. You don't have Jesus standing next to you in the flesh taking care of your every need.

But you do have something *better.*

I realize it's difficult to believe there's anything more beneficial than Jesus' physical presence. But there is. Jesus said so Himself.

That's right. In the hours just before He was crucified, He told His disciples that He would be leaving them and returning to His Father in heaven. When they expressed their sorrow and dismay, He said:

> *"And I will pray the Father, and He will give you another Helper, that He may abide with you forever—the Spirit of truth, whom the world cannot receive, because it neither sees Him nor knows Him; but you know Him, for He dwells with you and will be in you.....Nevertheless I tell you the truth. It is to your advantage that I go away; for if I do not go away, the Helper will not come to you; but if I depart, I will send Him to you."*

John 14:16-17, 16:7

To fully grasp the impact of this last statement, you have to realize that Jesus was talking to a group of men who had followed Him day and night for three years. They had seen His miracles. They had enjoyed perfect protection and provision at His hand.

Peter was sitting there among them. Can't you just imagine what was running through his mind? No doubt he was thinking of the first time Jesus had borrowed his boat. After He'd finished preaching from it, He'd said to Peter, "Grab your nets and we'll go catch us some fish." It was the middle of the day. Peter knew you couldn't catch fish in the daylight in that lake—the water was too clear. The fish would see the net and run from it.

But just to humor Him, Peter had done what Jesus said and ended up with a net-busting, boat-sinking load of fish. What a day!

Then there was the time Jesus healed Peter's mother-in-law of a deadly fever. Cured her instantly!

Even that didn't hold a candle to what happened on the Mount of Transfiguration. That day Peter had actually seen Moses and Elijah talking with Jesus. He had watched His body transfigure before his very eyes. He'd seen the shining cloud of glory and heard the awesome voice of Almighty God!

As those events passed through Peter's mind, he must have wondered, *How can it possibly be expedient or to my "advantage" for Jesus to go away?*

Knowing that question was in the heart of every one of His disciples, Jesus said, in essence, *"I know this is hard for you to believe, but trust Me on this. I'm not lying to you. It's better for you if I go away so that I can send the Holy Spirit to not only be with you, but to be in you!"*

The Power of God

It's been more than 2,000 years since Jesus foretold the importance of the Holy Spirit—and most of us are still struggling to fully believe it.

Theologically, we know it's true, and we thank God that we're born again and baptized in the Holy Ghost. But then we open our mouths and say things like, "If I could just feel Jesus' hand on my forehead, it would be easier for me to receive my healing."

Why is that?

I believe it's because we haven't truly appreciated the might and the ministry of the Holy Spirit. We haven't yet had a full revelation of Who this is that is living inside us.

Many Christians, for example, seem to think the first time the Holy Spirit did much of anything was on the Day of Pentecost. But that's not true. The Holy Spirit has been at work on this planet ever since the beginning.

Look at the Book of Genesis and you can see that for yourself. There in the first few verses we find:

> *"In the beginning God created the heaven and the earth. And the earth was without form, and void; and darkness was upon the face of the deep. And the spirit of God moved upon the face of the waters. And God said, Let there be light: and there was light."*
>
> Genesis 1:1-3

Think about that! The Holy Spirit was hovering, waiting to supply the power to create. Then the moment God spoke the Word, *"Light be!"* (literal Hebrew translation), the Spirit sprang into action and supplied the power to bring this universe into being.

That's how the Bible introduces us to the Holy Spirit!

You see, the Holy Spirit is the power of God. Every time you see God's power in action, you can be sure the Holy Spirit is on the scene.

When the Holy Spirit came on Samson, he single-handedly killed a thousand Philistine soldiers (see Judges 15:14-16). Can you imagine how embarrassing that must have been for the Philistines who escaped?

Some people get the idea that Samson was able to do those great exploits because he was a giant of a man. But he was really just an ordinary fellow. He only became extraordinary when the Spirit of God came on him.

The prophet Elijah was the same way. On his own, he was just as normal as you and me. He was once so frightened by the threats of a woman that he hid in the wilderness and asked God to kill him so he wouldn't have to face her.

But when the Holy Spirit came on him, Elijah was a power-house. He once called down fire from heaven, killed 400 prophets of Baal, and outran the king's chariot (drawn, no doubt, by the fastest horses in the nation of Israel). And he did it all in one day. (See 1 Kings 18-19.)

The Most Amazing Mind!

Don't get the idea from those examples that the Holy Spirit is simply a mindless source of raw power. Far from it! When He moves in on a situation, He does it with wisdom and understanding so vast that it staggers the human mind.

Isaiah 40:13 says of Him: *"Who hath directed the spirit of the Lord, or being his counselor hath taught him?"* Now go back and read how verse 12 further explains: *"Who hath measured the waters in the hollow of his hand, and meted out heaven with the span, and comprehended the dust of the earth in a measure, and weighed the mountains in scales, and the hills in a balance?"*

Consider for a moment what kind of mind could take a handful of water, weigh it and then compute all the moisture changes of the earth that would take place over untold thousands of years.

What kind of mind could take a handful of dust, weigh it, and then figure out how to form the earth—mountains and all—in such a way that it would always stay in perfect balance?

That's the kind of mind the Spirit of God has!

When He put this earth together, He did it so perfectly that it can travel 1,000 miles an hour in one direction and 10,000 miles an hour in another, both at the same time, without ever getting the slightest degree off course. He constructed it so that it could compensate for all the movement of the tides and all the use and abuse it would receive at the hands of man and still make its way through the heavens exactly on time.

Listen, this is the One Who is planning your life! This is the One Who dwells within you and walks within you. When you join yourself to the Lord, you become one spirit with Him (1 Corinthians 6:17). And He doesn't change or shrink up His abilities so He could fit them inside you.

No, if you're a born-again, Holy Spirit-baptized believer, He is everything *in you* that He has ever been. He has the same awesome power. He has the same astounding ability to compute, to comprehend and plan in infinite detail everything that has ever been—everything that now is—and everything that ever will be!

What's more, when you run into something you can't handle and you call on Him for help, He's not a million light years away. He's right there inside you! He's ready to supply you with whatever you need.

He's ready to be your comforter. He's ready to be your teacher and your trainer. He's ready to be your advocate, your standby, your counselor. He's ready to put His supernatural power and mind to work for you 24 hours a day.

A Perfect Gentleman

"Well then, why hasn't He helped me before now?" you ask. *"Heaven knows I've needed it!"*

He's been waiting for you to give Him something He can work with. He's been waiting there inside you just like He hovered over the face of the waters in Genesis, waiting for you to speak the Word of God in faith.

That's been His role since the beginning–to move on God's Word and deliver the power necessary to cause that Word to manifest in the earth. That's what He did at creation...and that's what He is commissioned to do for you.

But remember, He's your helper, not your dominator. If you're walking around talking doubt, unbelief and other worthless junk, He is severely limited. He won't slap His hand over your mouth and say, "You dummy, I don't care what you say, I'm going to bless you anyway."

No, the Holy Spirit is the perfect gentleman. He'll never force anything on you. He'll just wait quietly for you to open the door for Him to work.

So decide right now to start opening that door. Develop an awareness of the reality of the Holy Spirit within you. Stop spending all your time meditating on the problems you're facing and start spending it meditating on the power of the One inside you Who can solve the problems. In other words, start becoming more God-inside minded!

Do you know what will happen if you do that? All heaven will break loose in your life.

The Holy Spirit Within

Instead of walking around moaning about how broke you are and how you can't afford to give much to spread the gospel, you'll start thinking about the fact that the One with the power to bring God's Word to pass is living inside you, and you'll change your tune. You'll start saying things like, "God meets my needs according to His riches in glory, so I have plenty to meet my own needs and give to every good work!"

Then the Holy Spirit within you will go into action. He'll give you plans, ideas and inventions. He'll open doors of opportunity and then give you the strength and ability to walk through them.

Instead of sitting around wishing there was something you could do for your sick, unsaved neighbor, you'll march into his house, tell him about Jesus, and then lay hands on him fully expecting the Holy Spirit within you to release God's healing power and cause him to recover.

Instead of sitting around simply admiring the works of Jesus and reading about them each Sunday in church, you'll hit the streets and do those works yourself—and even greater works (see John 14:12). You'll stand up boldly and say:

> *"The Spirit of the LORD is upon Me, Because He has anointed Me, To preach the gospel to the poor; He has sent Me to heal the brokenhearted, To proclaim liberty to the captives And recovery of sight to the blind To set at liberty those who are oppressed; To proclaim the acceptable year of the LORD"*
>
> Luke 4:18-19

More Than You Can Think

"Wait a minute. Jesus spoke those words about Himself!"

Yes, He did. But He also said, *"...As my Father hath sent me, even so send I you"* (John 20:21).

You've been sent just like Jesus was. You've been sent to your family, your neighborhood, your workplace, your world to deliver the burden-removing, yoke-destroying power of God!

That's the reason God baptized you in the Holy Spirit. He intended for you to walk into a place and bring the power of God on the scene—the same power that enabled Samson to defeat the Philistines and make a fool out of the devil! The same power that enabled Elijah to call down fire from heaven and outrun the fastest horses in the country! The same power that enabled Jesus to heal the sick, raise the dead and calm the sea!

Can you imagine what all God could do in this earth if we'd just become God-inside minded enough to let that power flow?

No, you can't. For as the Apostle Paul said, He is *"able to do exceedingly abundantly above all that we ask or think, according to the power that works in us"* (Ephesians 3:20).

Maybe you've been waiting for God to do something in your life or in the lives of those around you. Maybe you've been saying, *"I know God is able to change this situation. I wonder why He doesn't do it?"* If so, read that last phrase again. It says He is able to do above what we can ask or think *according to the power that works in you!*

Start building your faith in that power. Instead of always gazing toward heaven saying, *"God, why don't You help me?"* look at yourself in the mirror and say, "The Spirit of God is living in me today and I expect Him to do wise, wonderful, amazing and miraculous things through me!"

Instead of meditating on your problems and natural inadequacies, get out your Bible and study the acts of the Holy Spirit from Genesis to Revelation. Start meditating on the power and sufficiency of the *Greater One* who lives and walks within you every moment of every day!

When you begin to realize what a dynamite team you two really are, you'll blast off into the realm of exceedingly above all that you can ask or think—and the devil will never be able to catch you.

Chapter 4

LIVING IN TWO PLACES AT ONCE

H ave you ever wished that you could just "runaway?" *If only there was someplace I could go to hide until all the problems just went away!*

Believe it or not—there *is* just such a place for dedicated, born again, spirit-filled believers! We have a secret place that is beyond human reasoning and scientific calculation. It's a place far above the problems that face us in this earth. It's similar to the place where eagles dare to go!

Where Eagles Dare to Go

During storms, the eagle rises above all turbulence by spreading his wings—locking them tight—and escapes the fury of an impact that could be devastating if faced head-on. The eagle has a hiding place that is in high places—sometimes known to be miles high.

We who are "in Christ" also have a "mile-high" strength and faith that the "world" knows nothing about.

Consider this promise from the Word:

> *"Have you not known? Have you not heard? The everlasting God, the Lord, The Creator of the ends of the earth, Neither faints nor is weary. His understanding is unsearchable. He gives power to the weak, And to those who have no might He increases strength. Even the youths shall faint and be weary,*

And the young men shall utterly fall, But those who wait upon the Lord Shall renew their strength; They shall mount up with wings like eagles, They shall run and not be weary, They shall walk and not faint."

Isaiah 40:28-31

The Greatest Mystery

Unfortunately, many Christians don't know what God's secret place is—where it is—or how to get there.

First, let's talk about what it is. Psalm 91 begins like this:

He who dwells in the secret place of the most High Shall abide under the shadow of the Almighty. I will say of the Lord, "He is my refuge and my fortress; My God, in Him I will trust."

If you continue reading you will find that this Psalm of protection has never been more relative than it is in the 21st century! "Under the shadow" means protected. It's God's protection in times of terrorism, disease, and disaster.

You and I can go to the *secret place* when we are deep in prayer and communion with God the Father. It's as though your spirit is so energized with the presence of God that you are no longer strongly aware of, or concerned with your body—or the circumstances around you.

The *secret place* is a holy place of worship, praise, and God's protection. You can enter this place while your body is anywhere—prison, hospital, lunch hour, or taking a walk. (Even at church!)

It's Like Heaven On Earth

You are a spirit—you live in a body. When your body dies, your spirit lives on, and goes directly to heaven!

So going to God's secret place is the closest thing to heaven that we can experience without physically dying.

Take a look at how the apostle Paul referred to this spiritual experience in 2 Corinthians 12:1-4:

"It is doubtless not profitable for me to boast. I will come to visions and revelations of the Lord: I know a man in Christ who fourteen years ago—whether in the body I do not know, or whether out of the body I do not know, God knows—such a one was caught up into the third heaven. And I know such a man—whether in the body or out of the body I do not know, God knows—how he was caught up into paradise and heard inexpressible words, which is not lawful for a man to utter."

Now I am not suggesting that you try to equal Paul's experiences with God, but this is a start in understanding the spiritual—secret place that you can have with the Father God. (This is the difference between born again believers and unbelievers. When faced with the storms of life, believers have a secret place to go.)

Ground Zero

Where do you live? Do you live on a planet called Earth?

I realize you may be thinking this is a strange thing to ask. But it's important. Because the answer to the question, *Where do you live?* will determine your outcome should there be another terrorist threat. It will determine your outcome should there be an unexpected outbreak of disease, or should another gunman begin randomly shooting people, or another horrible hurricane.

Where you live will determine your outcome in the next episode of fear.

The place where you actually live is only about 18 inches below your nose. Of course, I am referring to your inner self—the real you on the inside. Your spirit being is where you dwell and have life. It's where real life, true peace and happiness, takes place.

So in reality, you can leave your house in New York, or Texas, or Michigan and go to the other side of the world. And no matter where you go, your dwelling will go with you.

Every moment of every day our "baggage" also travels with us. Every doubt we have, every fear and ugly emotion that we could possibly have packed away deep inside ourselves—it's all with us and it goes wherever we go.

That's why the opening words of Psalm 91 are so powerful:

> *"He who dwells in the secret place of the Most High*
> *Shall abide under the shadow of the Almighty."*

How Do We Abide In God's Secret Place?

We get to the secret place by "saying" something!

Verse 2 of Psalm 91 gives us the key to this spiritual dwelling place: "I will say of the Lord, He is my refuge and my fortress; My God; in Him I will trust."

We say, or pray—or *forecast*—ourselves into God's secret dwelling place. In other words, we are the ones who determine where we dwell and everything that happens there. (Of course we won't get to *first base* without the blood sacrifice of Jesus.) So after we are born again (in Christ), we build our spirit with the Word—and then speak that Word.

What we experience day in and day out does not come from our heads. Neither does it come from what's going on around us. Our lives are not based on what's happening in New York City, Washington, D.C., Detroit, Afghanistan, or Iraq.

No.

Life—and every aspect of it—comes out of our spirit. Our *spirit man* is the determining factor. (*Spirit man* refers to both men and women.)

Because you and I are "in Christ," we have access to the secret place of the Most High. We can go to where the remaining promises of Psalm 91 apply to us:

> *"Surely He shall deliver you from the snare of the*
> *fowler And from the perilous pestilence. He shall*
> *cover you with His feathers And under his wings*
> *you shall take refuge: His truth shall be your shield*
> *and buckler. You shall not be afraid of the terror by*
> *night, Nor of the arrow that flies by day, Nor for the*

pestilence that walks in darkness, Nor of the destruc-
tion that lays waste at noonday. A thousand may fall
at your side, And ten thousand at your right hand;
But it shall not come near you."

Psalm 91:3-10

Angels Are In Charge

Yesterday is gone (along with five minutes ago). Even the angels of God cannot change the past. But if you understand how these mighty unseen heavenly beings operate you can get supernatural assistance for your future.

Angels are not little fat babies or women with long blonde hair and bows and arrows in their hands. The Bible describes them as great and mighty in strength and ability. And if you are a believer they are a vital part of your life.

Angels are "all ministering spirits sent forth to minister for those who will inherit salvation." Angels can become an active part of your personal future.[2]

Just think about that. God has created vast numbers of gloriously powerful spiritual beings for the express purpose of serving us and defending us against the evils of this world.

If we are going to abide in God's secret place, we can expect a supernatural protection from guardian angels!

Custom Built by God

Isaiah 54 gives us a phenomenal description of our secret place in God. It's His covenant of promise to us concerning our well-being in this lifetime.

The Most High God, Himself, is building us a house—a refuge, a safe haven, a secret place.

God's promise reads like this:

"In righteousness you shall be established; You shall
be far from oppression, for you shall not fear; And
from terror, for it shall not come near you. Indeed

44

they shall surely gather together but not because of Me. Whoever assembles against you shall fall for your sake. Behold, I have created the blacksmith Who blows the coals in the fire, Who brings forth an instrument for his work; And I have created the spoiler to destroy. No weapon that formed against you shall prosper."

Isaiah 54:8-10.

The key to being far from oppression, far from fear, and far from all acts of terror—is being established in God's Word, and abiding in God's secret place.

PSALM 25:14

The secret of the Lord is with those who fear Him, And He will show them His covenant.

Chapter 5

PSALM 91 IS REAL TODAY!

W hen our heart aches with grief—when our body is screaming at us in pain—when terror is exploding all around us—we can begin to *pray* and *declare*:

> *The Lord is my Shepherd, therefore I shall not want.*
> *Greater is He who is within me than he who is in the*
> *world. Jesus took on flesh and blood that He might*
> *destroy the devil and his power over me through*
> *death. Besides that, God is Love and He loves me,*
> *and there is no fear in Love, therefore, I have no fear.*
> *I have no torment. I refuse to be terrorized. I refuse*
> *to be paralyzed.*

That's how you dominate fear, instead of it dominating you. That's how you abide in the secret place of the Most High God.

The Bible says "the work of righteousness shall be peace [nothing missing and nothing broken in our lives]; and the effect of righteousness quietness and assurance forever."

Think about that for a moment. The work of righteousness is peace. The effect of righteousness is quietness and assurance.

Does that only apply as long as the Islamic terrorists stay in some other country on the other side of the world?

No.

The peace, the quietness, and assurance of righteousness are forever!

The Bible goes on to say, *"My people shall* dwell *in a peaceful habitation, In secure* dwellings, *and in quiet resting places."*

49

Peace, Quietness, and Assurance

We can live in peace, quietness, and assurance every day of our life. We are the righteousness of God in Christ Jesus. If we will allow His righteousness to develop and work in our life it will be as an invisible shield of blessing around us everywhere we go—at home, at work, when we're asleep, when we're awake. It is our "shield," of protection.

Take this word to heart, put it into practice and learn how to live in the secret place of the Most High. Claim your place in the secret place of the Most High God.

Even when terror strikes close to home —it will remain far from you.

God's Supernatural Protection

The Word of God is filled with accounts of supernatural protection for God's people. It's no problem for God to bring you out of a fiery furnace or shut the mouth of a lion. He has proven time and again He's well able to get the job done no matter what the circumstances.

But God's protection is not automatic. There are things you have to do in order for God to be your refuge. There are choices you have to make.

If we choose to live in sin, we probably won't live a long and healthy life. If we choose to follow the devil, we will receive the same reward he does. (And that's not something we want.)

Instead, we desire to be like the person in Psalm 91. He has made the choice to dwell, or abide, in the secret place of the Most High. He makes his abode there, in order to receive the protection that Psalm 91 promises. His dependence is on God. And he stays stable and fixed under God's shadow by being obedient. The good things of God—the blessings and deliverance from the curse—are only for the obedient. They are not for everybody.

The good things belong to those who do what God says—to those who seek Him.

Living *on purpose* with God the Father is the only safe way to live!

He Is My Refuge!

Another important thing to notice about Psalm 91 is that we have to learn to *speak* our faith. "I will say of the Lord, He is my Refuge and my Fortress; My God, in Him I will trust!"

Faith has to be in two places—in your heart and in your mouth. First, you must agree in your head with what the Word says in order to get it into your heart. Then, it has to be in your heart to such a degree that it overflows. That only comes by spending time seeking God and His Word.

Then as Jesus said, "Out of the abundance of the heart the mouth speaks."[7]

We have to be able to say in faith, *"He is my refuge and my fortress!"* You have to trust God for your protection and say so!

Today, we need a vitally important "lifeline" from Psalm 91: "You shall not be afraid." Fear has to go. We will not be held hostage by fear.

Go to the Secret Place

If someone is being mean to you, or you are having trouble—go to God's *secret place*!

When you need to feel the love and protection of God your Father—go to the secret place.

When you feel bad—go to God's *secret place*. Instead of arguing, complaining, or doing wrong things—go to God's *secret place*. That's where there is real life, safety, and lots of joy!

In the secret place you can pray heavenly words. You can *pray in the spirit*. You can speak mysteries to God, in Jesus name!

The Bible says it like this:

> *"I will pray with the spirit, and I will also pray with the understanding"*
>
> 1 Corinthians14:15.

There is not a magic formula for being filled with the Holy Spirit. Just ask the Father God, in Jesus name. This should be your deepest, most heartfelt prayer.

Then just begin to pray heavenly words—inspired by the Holy Spirit.

In The "Zone"

Athletes that are very focused on their sport are said to be in a "zone." They don't notice the crowd or even the other players. They just *see* a goal line, or a perfect play, or a great performance. It's as if they were in a *secret place*. (In God's secret place we will just *see* Him, not our problems.)

The Bible encourages us like this:

> *"I press toward the goal for the prize of the upward call of God in Christ Jesus."*
>
> Philippians 3:14.

Your Suit of Armor

You can "stand against the wiles of the devil" with God's spiritual armor. (See Ephesians 6:10-17.)

God's *secret place* is where you can put on your spiritual *Armor*.

Armor is a word that is used to define clothes of protection. Like a helmet and a shield. You can't *see* God's armor, just like you can't *see* the powerful words that you speak in Jesus name. But this armor is very real.

How do we put on God's armor?

When you are praying in the secret place—use your spiritual "eye of faith" while you read the Word out loud.

God's Word is amazing! Study the whole 91st Psalm. Read it out loud. Say it out loud. Memorize it. The amazing thing is that it even applies to this evil world of *terrorism*. God's Word is awesome!

This Is Not the Time For Weak Faith

These are serious days. It's no time to be sitting on the fence and being double-minded. We can *decide* where we are going to dwell—where we are going to put our trust.

Dependence on God requires spending time with Him and His Word, because faith comes by hearing and hearing by the Word of God. By spending time in the Word, we will become fully persuaded that God is faithful. This assurance gives peace and replaces every fear.

Fifty years ago no one would have thought biological weapons and epidemic diseases would be a threat today. But we have the antidote right here. God will deliver us when we abide in Him, trust Him and say so.

When you hear threatening reports, talk back! Say, *"No, that's not coming to me, or to my house!"* Don't let the enemy talk you out of your healing and protection. Receive all the good things God has declared for you in Psalm 91.

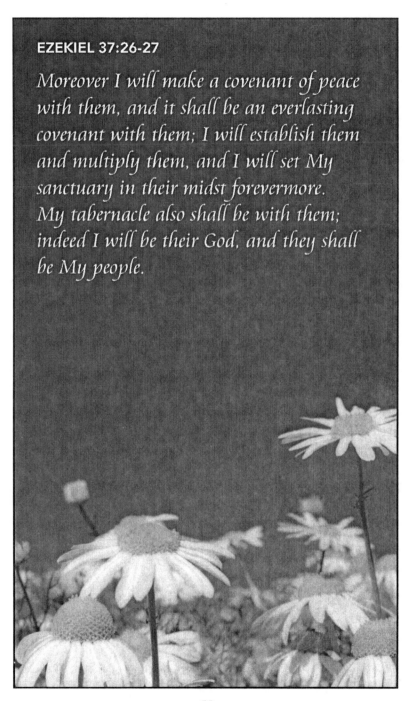

EZEKIEL 37:26-27

Moreover I will make a covenant of peace with them, and it shall be an everlasting covenant with them; I will establish them and multiply them, and I will set My sanctuary in their midst forevermore. My tabernacle also shall be with them; indeed I will be their God, and they shall be My people.

Chapter 6

PRAYING HEAVEN'S SECRETS

Have you ever prayed and wondered if God really heard you? Have you ever tried praying to God without really knowing what to say?

Of course, we always want to pray by quoting Scriptures, like Jesus did when He was tempted by the devil; Matthew 4:4. But sometimes we just don't know what to pray! Don't be discouraged; there is a fail-proof way to pray that guarantees results every time. It's through praying in the Spirit, or praying in tongues. This is the way to pray Heaven's secrets.

Don't be afraid of the word, tongues. (It is not spooky or weird, as some have distorted this wonderful blessing of God.) The word "tongues" is simply an old English word for "language." So you can say with complete accuracy that praying in tongues is praying in a heavenly language.

When you tap into this awesome spiritual gift, not only are you able to pray the perfect prayer, but you are worshipping God in spirit and in truth, (John 4:24). Plus, this kind of prayer is the doorway to the supernatural gifts of the Holy Spirit and miracles.

It's important to understand that the ability to pray in tongues is from God. When you pray in tongues in your personal prayer time, you are communicating with God directly and not publically. It's also important to know that there is a difference between your personal prayer language of tongues and the public delivery of the *gift* of tongues.

First Corinthians 14:14-15 says,

"For if I pray in an unknown tongue, my spirit pray, but my understanding is unfruitful. What is it then? I will pray with the spirit, and I will pray with the understanding also: I will sing with the spirit, and I will sing with the understanding also."

Your prayer in the Spirit is just between you and the Father, so you don't have to worry about giving an interpretation to anyone else, although you can ask God to give you the interpretation of what you just prayed.

Scripture also reveals that praying in the Spirit is a tool of intercession.

Romans 8:26-28 says:

"Likewise the Spirit also help our infirmities: for we know not what we should pray for as we ought: but the Spirit itself make intercession for us with groanings which cannot be uttered. And he that search the hearts know what is the mind of the Spirit, because he make intercession for the saints according to the will of God. And we know that all things work together for good to them that love God, to them who are the called according to his purpose."

This passage is often misunderstood. Religion has used it to justify the bad things that happen to people, saying that "all things work together for good." While God can take your mess and turn it into a masterpiece, I don't believe that catastrophe, disaster and tragedy happen for your good or to teach you something. This scripture is talking about prayer and, specifically, praying in the Spirit.

Pray the Perfect Prayer

Since the Spirit of God knows the mind and will of the Father, when you intercede in tongues, you pray the perfect will of God. Satan can't interfere with your prayers when you pray in the Spirit because he doesn't know what you are saying! As a matter of fact, not even *you* can get in the way of your prayers when you pray this way. Since you don't know what you are saying, fear, doubt and unbelief can't stop your prayer from coming to pass. That's why the Apostle Paul says that all things work together for good to those who are called according to God's purpose—to those who pray the perfect will of God.

Don't let anyone talk you out of your God-given right to pray in tongues. It is not a gift that passed away with the last apostle, and it is not spooky or weird. The disciples all received the gift of tongues on the day of Pentecost (Acts 2:1-4), and this gift is available to you, too! Just pray for the baptism of the Holy Spirit and open your mouth in faith, speaking whatever comes up out of your spirit. You'll begin to pray more confidently and more effectively, secure in the knowledge that God will hear and answer your prayers.

Who is the Holy Spirit?

The subject of the Holy Spirit is one of the most misunderstood and misinterpreted subjects among Christians and non–Christians. Many people are afraid to hear sermons about the Holy Spirit because of incorrect teachings they may have received in the past. The topic of speaking in tongues and the gifts of the Spirit are often shunned as a result. However, the Holy Spirit is real. He desires to work through you so that you can experience the power that God ordained every Christian to have and use in these last days.

Gaining an understanding of who the Holy Spirit is, and who He is not, is critical in order to experience His presence and power. The Holy Spirit is *not* a feeling or an emotion. Although His presence can stir up emotions within you, He actually is the third person of the Trinity God the Father, God the Son and God the Holy Spirit. When you receive Jesus Christ as your Lord and Savior, the Holy Spirit comes to live in your heart; it becomes His dwelling place. As you learn to yield to Him, you will find yourself walking out God's plan for your life. In addition, you will experience supernatural power and breakthrough like never before.

Jesus explains the function of the Holy Spirit in John 16:7, "Nevertheless I tell you the truth: It is expedient for you that I go away: for if I go not away, the Comforter will not come unto you; but if I depart, I will send him unto you." Jesus knew He would have to leave in order for the Holy Spirit to come to the earth. Now that the Holy Spirit is here, and dwelling in every member of the body of Christ, the power of God can flow to an even greater extent than when Jesus walked the earth!

The Holy Spirit is the motivator, energizer and operator of every revealed plan or vision from God. He is also the revealer of the hidden treasures of the Kingdom of God and holds the key to the inheritance of the saints. He is the most valuable asset to Christian living, and yet many times, Believers don't know enough about Him to really take advantage of what He can do in their lives.

Praying During the End Times

Since we are living in the Last Days, it is going to be imperative that you know how to distinguish the Holy Spirit's voice. That "hunch" or inner feeling you have inside, that is either directing you or telling you not to do something, is the Holy Spirit.

You can develop a discernment of His voice through studying and meditating on the Word of God. He will never say anything to you that doesn't line up with the written Word, so studying the Bible is essential to your recognizing His voice.

Praying in tongues also helps to sharpen your spiritual discernment and awareness of Him. It may take some time to become proficient in recognizing His voice, but as you develop, pay attention to whether or not you have peace in your spirit about something you are about to do. If you don't, most likely the Holy Spirit is warning you not to proceed.

When you acknowledge the Holy Spirit and commune with Him on a daily basis, He will show you mysteries and the secret plans of God for your life. Jeremiah 33:3 says, *"Call unto me, and I will answer thee, and show thee great and mighty things, which thou know not."* He will guide you into your destiny when you allow Him to direct your decisions.

When you call on the Holy Spirit, you may say, "Holy Spirit, I don't know what to do in this situation, but I know You know the answer. Show me what to do." Spend some time praying in the Spirit and then wait on Him until you hear Him speak to you about it. When you call, He will answer.

You can cultivate your relationship with the Holy Spirit by praising God, praying and singing spiritual songs (Ephesians 5:19). Doing these things helps to build your spirit and makes you more sensitive to His presence. Invite Him into every situation and atmosphere in which you find yourself. When you acknowledge Him this way, He will be able to move in your life.

Since the Holy Spirit was sent to help guide and direct your life, it is important that you set aside time every day to fellowship with Him. Talk with Him as you would a close friend or family member. Let Him know your concerns and confess the Scriptures. He will give you the revelation, insight and enlightenment you need to lead you into the good life God has prepared for you.

Developing a relationship with the Holy Spirit is going to cost you something. It will mean getting up to pray when you don't feel like it and letting go of old habits and mindsets that oppose God's Word. But when you create an environment in which the Holy Spirit can dwell, you will reap the rich rewards of your relationship with Him. Are you willing to pay the price?

It's Controversial!

Speaking in tongues is the most talked about phenomena in Christianity. Pentecostalism and the Charismatic movement have brought speaking in tongues to the forefront. Believe it or not, these branches of Christianity are without doubt the fastest growing segments of Christianity. These movements are impacting the world even more than the reformation did.

Yet with all the talk about speaking in tongues, few understand what it's all about. It is the least understood subject among believers. People will be surprise to find that the Bible mentions speaking in tongues thirty-five times. That is a lot, so this subject should not be cast lightly aside as unimportant to the Church. God does not fill His book with things of minor importance.

Many people who have never spoken in tongues speak as though they're experts in this field, when in reality they teach only from theory.

Who should know more about tongues: those who speak in tongues or those who don't? Well, shouldn't we learn from those who do speak in tongues!? Since I do speak in tongues, I feel that I can bring scriptural wisdom with experience and help to clarify common misunderstandings and show the importance and benefits of speaking in tongues.

What Good Is Praying in the Spirit?

The Apostle Paul writes, "He who speaks in tongues edifies himself...I would like every one of you to speak in tongues" (1 Corinthians 14:4-5). With these positive statements about tongues, why do so few Christians speak in tongues? I believe the answer is because there is very little sound, logical and scriptural teaching as to the scope and value of speaking in tongues.

I have shared my testimony several times on how God saved me and filled me with the Holy Spirit with the evidence of speaking in new tongues. After each time, the number one question asked was on speaking in tongues. One frequently asked question is, "What does speaking in tongues do for you anyway?"

I will always explain, "It does exactly what the Bible says it does: He who speaks in tongues edifies himself." The word "edify" means to "build up" or "charge up"—much like charging up a battery. We all need a spiritual charge. All of us at times feel spiritually drained. One of God's ways to charge up your spirit is through speaking in tongues.

It's a Heavenly Language

Many people inaccurately define speaking in tongues as "speaking gibberish" or "talking nonsense." The truth is, speaking in tongues is the most intelligent, perfect language in the universe. It is God's language.

What language do you suppose people speak in heaven? Languages are given their name based on the countries they come from. For example, English comes from England. Spanish comes from Spain. Italian comes from Italy.

Well, where does tongues come from? It comes from Heaven! Tongues is the heavenly language. Here on earth Paul says, *"For anyone who speaks in tongues does not speak to men but to God. Indeed, no one understands him; he utters mysteries with his spirit"* (v. 2).

Jesus said that those who believe in Him will "speak in new tongues" (Mark 16:17). The word "new" means appearing for the first time. No one had spoken these languages before. Contrary to bad theology, tongues is not an ability given to preach the gospel in the language of foreigners. This would make tongues "old" languages. It's only appropriate that "new tongues" should be spoken by those of the "new birth." It's natural and normal to speak in the language of your birth. We are born again from above, therefore we should speak the language from above—that language is called "new tongues."

Should Tongues be Understood?

The first ones to speak in tongues were the disciples. This occurred on the day of Pentecost. People often think that on this day the disciples were speaking human languages, because the people could understand what they were saying.

I don't believe this is true because there was a two-fold miracle taking place on this day: the miracle of speaking and hearing: The first miracle was the speaking in tongues. The second miracle was the enabling of some to understand the tongues. Not everyone understood the tongues, because some onlookers made fun of the disciples and accused them of being drunk (Acts 2:13); this clearly shows that they did not understand the tongues. And the ones who did understand the tongues were confused because each one heard only their own native language not the languages of the other people (v. 6).

The Bible tells us that there were over fourteen foreigners representing many nations, speaking different languages. Yet each person heard the disciples praising God in their own language. They exclaimed, *"How is it that each of us hears them in his own native language?"* (v. 8) They could not figure out how this was possible.

It's clear that the disciples were not "preaching" the gospel in tongues, they were instead *"declaring the wonders of God"* (v. 11). They were not speaking "to men but to God" (1 Corinthians 14:2). The people were simply listening in on their praises to God. It wasn't until Peter stood up to speak to the crowd in one common language that the gospel was preached. So tongues are not supernatural human languages given to the apostles so they could preach in languages they did not naturally learn.

The disciples were not speaking human languages; they were speaking in unknown tongues. But God enabled those whose hearts were opened to understand what the disciples were saying. Sometimes this happens today. You see, the miracle was in the hearing of the people.

The Baptism with the Holy Spirit

Let's look carefully at the first scriptural account of speaking in tongues:

> *"When the day of Pentecost came, they were all together in one place. Suddenly a sound like the blowing of a violent wind came from heaven and filled the whole house where they were sitting. They saw what seemed to be tongues of fire that separated and came to rest on each of them. All of them were filled with the Holy Spirit and began to speak in other tongues as the Spirit enabled them."*
>
> Acts 2:1-4.

This experience is what John the Baptist and Jesus called the baptism with the Holy Spirit. This was the fulfillment of Jesus promise, "In a few days you will be baptized with the Holy Spirit"

(Acts 1:5). Every Christian believes in baptizing in water. But few accept the 2nd baptism—the baptism with the Holy Spirit. Since you were willing to be baptized in water, shouldn't you also be willing to be baptized in the Holy Spirit?

Theologians often confuse the baptism with the Holy Spirit with salvation. They often regard these two experiences as being the same. This confuses believers. They incorrectly assume that salvation is the same as the baptism with the Holy Spirit. The Bible clearly teaches that the baptism with the Holy Spirit is a separate experience from salvation and comes after a person is saved, although it can occur at the time of salvation.

The story of the Samaritan converts plainly proves this (see Acts 8:5-25). Philip preached to them about Christ. The people joyfully accepted the gospel and were born again. They confirmed their faith by being baptized as well. Yet, despite the fact that these folks were truly saved, Philip called for the apostles to come and pray for them that they would receive the Holy Spirit. It is clear from this story that being saved is not the same as receiving the fullness of the Holy Spirit. (Although the Holy Spirit is definitely involved in salvation.)

Another biblical story illustrates this fact (see Acts 19:1-7). Paul met some disciples of John the Baptist. He thought they were believers in the Lord Jesus, because they talked so much about repentance. Paul, unaware that they were only disciples of John, yet knowing something was missing in these men, asked them an obvious question, "Did you receive the Holy Spirit when you believed?"

The question itself proves that Paul, including the early church, believed that it was possible to be a believer in Jesus without having received the Holy Spirit. If receiving the Holy Spirit was automatic at conversion, then why did Paul asked the question, "Did you receive the Holy Spirit when you believed?"

The Physical Evidence

The physical proof of the baptism with the Holy Spirit is the same evidence that the disciples had: speaking in tongues. You may have other evidences as well, but the one evidence you should have is speaking in tongues.

There are five examples in the Bible of people receiving the baptism in the Holy Spirit (see Acts 2:4; 8:17; 9:17; 10:44; 19:6).

In three out of the five examples we are told that specific signs took place. In the other two examples, the manifestation of physical signs taking place are implied, but not mentioned. Based on these two cases we cannot build any solid evidence as to what should happen when someone is baptized with the Holy Spirit. However, based on the other three examples we can build a good, solid case as to what should happen when someone is baptized in the Spirit.

We are told in these three examples that certain physical manifestations took place. In each case, more than one physical sign took place, which teaches us that there are usually more than one sign taking place when people are baptized in the Holy Spirit. Yet, there is one sign—and only one sign—that is common to all three examples. The identical sign was speaking in tongues. Based on this observation we can conclude that the standard sign of the baptism in the Holy Spirit is speaking in tongues.

Speaking in tongues is the physical, biblical evidence that one is baptized in the Holy Spirit. We should not settle for anything less than the scriptural evidence.

If you haven't been baptized in the Holy Spirit, seek God about it and pray in faith. God never lets a thirsty soul go dry.

Do All Speak in Tongues?

Someone may say, "How can anyone say that all Christians should speak in tongues considering the apostle Paul's words, 'Do all speak in tongues?'? (1 Corinthians 12:30).

In this passage, Paul is talking about public ministry gifts that are manifested in the church. He is not talking about tongues as the initial sign of the baptism in the Spirit, nor is he talking about tongues as a private, devotional, prayer language.

You can recognize this by simply looking at the language Paul uses concerning speaking in tongues. In this chapter he calls speaking in tongues "different kinds of tongues" (see 12:10,28). "Different kinds" means "not the usual." The usual kind of speaking in tongues is a language no man understands or interprets. However, speaking in "different kinds" of tongues enables the speaker or someone else to receive the meaning of the tongue by the Holy Spirit and thereby interpreting it.

So when Paul ask the question, "Do all speak in tongues?", he is referring to the public manifestation of tongues which enables a person gifted in interpretation to speak out the meaning of the tongue. Not all have been given this gift of "different kinds" of tongues.

In the fourteenth chapter of this epistle, Paul corrects the misuse of tongues in the church. He told them to stop the practice gathering "the whole church [so] everyone [can] speak in tongues" (v. 23).

Notice carefully that the "whole church" was gathered and that "everyone" was speaking in tongues. This clearly shows us that everyone in the Corinthian church was speaking in tongues. Most of them should have allowed those gifted in the "different kinds" of tongues to exercise their gift, and the rest should simply "keep quiet in the church and speak to himself and God" (v. 28).

I encourage you to seek the scriptural evidence of the baptism with the Holy Spirit, and to settle for nothing but the Lord's best for your life. (See Luke 11:13.)

2 CORINTHIANS 1:20

For all the promises of God in Him are Yes, and in Him Amen, to the glory of God through us.

Chapter 7

A FORECAST FOR HEALTH AND HEALING

G od has given us a powerful method to obtain His healing promises, and it's up to us to use it. That method is confession. Confession is when you speak in agreement with the "Word of God" out loud.

The word confession is equal to other action Bible words like profess, declare, foretell, proclaim, and prophesy. I like to say confession is your personal forecast of God's Word.

Words are spiritual containers that release either fear or faith. Every time you speak, you are activating spiritual forces that will affect your life. Your spiritual, mental, and physical health is dependent on saying and praying what God has promised in His Word. (We were created that way!)

Similar to the law of gravity, the law of confession will work for anyone who will get involved with it. Many Christians who have been defeated in life are defeated because they believe and confess the wrong things. They don't realize that their words are activating a spiritual law that is working against them. We must understand the law of confession if we want things to work for us.

We have been given access to the power of God through our words, (which are also weapons against the enemy).

Satan is constantly applying pressure to our minds in order to get us to quit in these last days; however, we don't have to allow hard times or pressure to defeat us. We can use the Word of God as a weapon against the enemy, and win!

In order to be victorious over the attacks of the enemy, we must think, believe, and speak in line with God's Word. In fact, storing the Word in our hearts is vital, because we are constantly storing "something" in our hearts. Out of our hearts will come blessing and healing or sickness and defeat. (Luke 6:45.)

> *If you can believe, all things are possible to those who believe."*
>
> Mark 9:23

Faith is the force that must be in operation in order for our confessions to come to pass. Sometimes people confess God's Word religiously, mechanically, and out of fear. However, these types of confessions don't accomplish anything. We must believe and expect that the things we confess from the Bible are coming to pass as we pray and speak them.

We can look to God as an example of how faith-filled words cause things to manifest in the natural realm. In the biblical account of how God created the earth, the Word says that He spoke and whatever He spoke came into existence, (Genesis 1).

God's words are full of faith, which is what caused them to become actual physical substance. The things we see in this earth today, from the sky to the trees, are the result of words that were spoken by God.

The same creative power that God possesses has been invested in us. As spiritual beings who possess the nature of God, we have the ability to speak things into existence just like God did. This isn't some mystical, New Age idea; it's Scriptural. When Jesus walked the earth, He imitated His Father by speaking what the Father spoke. He saw results everywhere He went. Likewise, we must be imitators of God, who think, act, and speak like Him. (Ephesians 5:1, and Romans 4:17.)

When we speak His Words, we release His creative ability into the earth, and something always happens. When we believe beyond a shadow of a doubt that the words we speak will come to pass, we will see the manifestation of what we are speaking, (Mark 11:22-23).

Confessing God's Word is so powerful because every time we hear ourselves speaking the Scriptures, we are actually planting faith in our hearts. The more we become established on the Word of God through speaking it on a consistent basis, the more our faith will grow. And faith, when acted upon, will always produce the desired results.

There shouldn't be a day that passes that the Believer does not speak the Word of God. It's the Word that strengthens our faith, and releases the power of God into our situations and circumstances. By making daily confessions, we frame our world with the Word of God, shut the devil out of our lives, and plant faith in our hearts. It is the key to victory and supernatural manifestation.

God's Prescription for Divine Health

There is a medicine so powerful it can cure every sickness and disease known to man. It has no dangerous side effects. It is safe even in massive doses. And when taken daily according to directions, it can prevent illness altogether and keep you in vibrant health.

Does that sound too good to be true? It's not. I can testify to you by the Word of God and by my own experience that such a supernatural medicine exists. Even more importantly, it is available to you every moment of every day.

You don't have to call your doctor to get it. You don't even have to drive to the pharmacy. All you must do is reach for your Bible, open to Proverbs 4:20-24 and follow the instructions you find there:

> *"My son, give attention to my words; Incline your ear to my sayings. Do not let them depart from your eyes; Keep them in the midst of your heart; For they are life to those who find them, And health to all their flesh. Keep your heart with all diligence, For out of it spring the issues of life. Put away from you a deceitful mouth, And put perverse lips far from you."*

As simple as they might sound, those four verses contain the supernatural prescription to divine health. It's a powerful prescription that will work for anyone who will put it to work.

If you have received healing by the laying on of hands, following this prescription will help you maintain that healing. If you have believed for healing, but are experiencing lingering symptoms, it will help you stand strong until you are completely symptom-free. And if you are healthy now, it will help you stay that way—not just for a day or a week, but for the rest of your life!

Powerful Medicine

To understand how this prescription works, you must realize that the Word of God is more than just good information. It actually has life in it. As Jesus said in John 6:63, *"It is the Spirit who gives life; the flesh profits nothing. The words that I speak to you are spirit, and they are life."*

Every time you take the Word into your heart, believe it and act on it, the very LIFE of God Himself, is released in you. You may have read the healing scriptures over and over again. You may know them as well as you know your own name. Yet every time you read them or hear them preached, they bring you a fresh dose of God's healing power. Each time, they bring life to you and deliver God's medicine to your flesh.

That's because the Word is like a seed. Hebrews 4:12 says it is *"alive and full of power—making it active, operative, energizing and effective..." (The Amplified Bible).* It actually carries within it the power to fulfill itself.

When you planted the Word about the new birth in your heart, then believed and acted on it, that Word released within you the power to be born again. By the same token, when you plant the Word about healing in your heart, believe and act on it, that Word will release God's healing power in you.

You may say, "I've met people who know the Bible from cover to cover and still can't get healed!"

No doubt you do. But if you'll look back at God's prescription, you'll find it doesn't say anything about "knowing" the Bible. It says, *attend* to the Word.

When you attend to something, you give your attention to it. You make it top priority. You set aside other things so you can focus on it. When a nurse is attending to a patient, she constantly looks after him. She doesn't just leave him lying alone in his hospital room while she goes shopping. If someone asks her about her patient, she doesn't feel it's sufficient to say, "Oh, yes. I know him."

In the same way, if you're attending to the Word, you won't leave it lying unopened on the coffee table all day. You won't spend your day focusing your attention on other things.

On the contrary, you'll do what Proverbs 4 says to do. You'll continually incline your ear to God's Word.

Inclining your ear includes more than just putting your physical ears in a position to hear the Word being preached (although that, in itself, is very important). It also requires you to actively engage with God's Word, to believe it and obey it.

In fact, *The Amplified Bible* translates Proverbs 4:20, this way: *"My son, attend to my words; consent and submit to my sayings."* Submitting to the Word means making adjustments in your life. Say, for example, you hear the Word in Philippians 4:4 that you are to *"rejoice in the Lord always."*

If you've been doing a lot of griping and complaining, you'll have to change in order to submit to that Word. You'll have to repent and alter your behavior.

Take as Directed

In addition to inclining your ear to the Word of God, the Proverbs 4 prescription also says you must keep it before your eyes and not let it depart from your sight. In Matthew 6:22-23, Jesus reveals why that's so important. He says, "The lamp of the body is the eye. If therefore your eye is good, your whole body will be full of light. [23] But if your eye is bad, your whole body will be full of darkness. If therefore the light that is in you is darkness, how great *is* that darkness!"

Your eyes are the gateway to your body. If your eye (or your attention) is on the darkness, or the sickness that is in your body, there will be no light to expel it. If, however, the eyes of your heart are trained strictly on the Word, your whole body will eventually be filled with light, and healing will be the result.

Granted, it isn't easy to keep your attention centered on the Word like that. It takes real effort and commitment. It may require getting up a little earlier in the morning or turning off the television at night. But I urge you to do whatever it takes to take God's medicine exactly as directed.

It Won't Work Any Other Way!

It really shouldn't be a big surprise. After all, we wouldn't expect natural medication to work for us if we didn't take it as prescribed.

No rational person would set a bottle of pills on the night stand and expect those pills to heal them.

No one would call the doctor and say, "Hey, doc! These pills don't work. I've carried them with me everywhere I go—I keep them in the car with me, I set them on my desk at work, I even have them next to me when I sleep at night—but I don't feel any better."

That would be ridiculous. Yet, spiritually speaking, some people do it all the time. They cry and pray and beg God to heal them, all the while ignoring the medicine He's provided. (They might take a quick dose on Sunday when they go to church, but the rest of the week they don't take time for the Word at all!)

Why do people who love God and believe the Bible act that way? I think it's because they don't understand how putting the Word in their heart can affect their physical bodies. They don't see how something spiritual can change something natural.

If you'll read the Bible, however, you'll see that spiritual power has been affecting this physical world ever since time began. In fact, it was spiritual power released in the form of God's Word that brought this natural world into existence in the first place.

When you realize that God's Word is the force that originally brought into being everything you can see and touch—including your physical body—it's easy to believe that the Word is still capable of changing your body today. It makes perfect sense!

God Has Already Spoken!

You might say, "I'd have no problem at all believing God's Word would heal me if He'd speak to me out loud like He did in Genesis, but He hasn't!"

No, and He probably won't either. God no longer has to thunder His Word down at us from heaven. These days He lives in the hearts of believers, so He speaks to us from the inside instead of the outside.

What's more, when it comes to covenant issues like healing, we don't even have to wait on Him to speak.

He has already said, *"...By [Jesus'] stripes ye were healed"* (I Peter 2:24). He has already said, *"...I am the Lord that healeth thee"* (Exodus 15:26). He has already said, *"The prayer of faith shall save the sick, and the Lord shall raise him up..."* (James 5:15).

God has already done His part. So we must do ours. We must take the Word He has spoken, put it inside us and let it change us from the inside out.

You see, everything—including healing—starts inside you. Your future is literally stored up in your heart. As Jesus said, "A good man out of the good treasure of his heart brings forth good things, and an evil man out of the evil treasure brings forth evil things" (Matthew 12:35).

That means if you want external conditions to be better tomorrow, you'd better start changing your internal condition today. You'd better start taking the Word of God and depositing it in your heart just like you deposit money in the bank. Then you can make withdrawals on it whenever you need it. When sickness attacks your body, you can tap into the healing Word you've put inside you and run that sickness off!

Exactly How Do You Do That?

You open your mouth and speak — not words of sickness and disease, discouragement and despair, but words of healing and life, faith and hope. You follow the last step of God's divine prescription and *"Put away from you a deceitful mouth, And put perverse lips far from you"* (verse 24).

In short, you speak the Words of God and call yourself healed in Jesus' Name.

Initially, that may not be easy for you to do. But you must do it anyway because for the faith to work it must be in two places—in your heart and in your mouth. *"For with the heart man believeth unto righteousness; and with the mouth confession is made unto salvation"* (Romans 10:10).

Some people say faith will move mountains. But, the scriptural truth is, faith won't even move a molehill for you unless you release it with the words of your mouth.

The Lord Jesus told us that "whoever says to this mountain, 'Be removed and be cast into the sea,' and does not doubt in his heart, but believes that those things he says will be done, he will have whatever he says," (Mark 11:23). Notice the word *"say"* appears three times in that verse while the word *believe* appears only once. Obviously, Jesus wanted us to know that our words are crucial.

It's also important to note that He did not instruct us to talk *about* the mountain, He instructed us to talk *to* it! If we're going to obey Him, we must talk to the mountain of sickness and cast it out of our lives. Instead of saying, "I'm healed," most Christians say, "I'm sick," and reinforce the sickness or disease.

Abraham went around calling himself the Father of Nations for years even though he was as childless as could be. Why did he do it? Because *"he believed...God, who gives life to the dead and calls those things which do not exist as though they did"* (Romans 4:17). He was *"fully persuaded that, what [God] had promised, he was able also to perform"* (verse 21).

You see, Abraham wasn't "trying" to believe God. He wasn't just mentally assenting to it. He had immersed himself in God's Word until that Word was more real to him than the things he could see. It didn't matter to him that he was 100 years old. It didn't matter to him that Sarah was far past the age of childbearing and that she had been barren all her life. All that mattered to him was what God said, because he knew His Word was true.

If you don't have that kind of faith for healing right now, then stay in the Word until you get it! After all, *"faith comes by hearing, and hearing by the word of God"* (Romans 10:17).

Read, study, meditate, listen to tapes, watch videos of good, and faith-filled teaching, until God's Word about healing is more real to you than the symptoms in your body.

Keep on keeping on until, like Abraham, you stagger not at the promise of God through unbelief, but grow strong in faith as you give praise and glory to God. (Romans 4:20, *The Amplified Bible.*)

Having Done All...Stand!

As you put God's prescription for health to work in your life, don't be discouraged if you don't see immediate results. Although many times healing comes instantly, there also are times when it takes place more gradually.

So don't let lingering symptoms cause you to doubt. After all, when you go to the doctor, you don't always feel better right away. The medication he gives you often takes some time before it begins to work. But you don't allow the delay to discourage you. You just follow the doctor's orders and expect to feel better soon. Really you are "treating" your spirit that is the source of supernatural life and health for your physical body.

Release that same kind of confidence in God's medicine. Realize that the moment you begin to take it, the healing process begins. Keep your expectancy high and make up your mind to continue standing on the Word until you can see and feel the total physical effects of God's healing power.

When the devil whispers words of doubt and unbelief to you, when he suggests that the Word is not working, deal with those thoughts immediately. Cast them down (see II Corinthians 10:5).

Speak out loud if necessary and say, "Devil, I rebuke you. I bind you from my mind. I will not believe your lies. God has sent His Word to heal me, and His Word never fails. That Word went to work in my body the instant I believed it, so as far as I am concerned, my days of sickness are over. I declare that Jesus bore my sickness, weakness and pain, and I am forever free."

Then, *"having done all to stand, stand"* until your healing is fully manifested (see Ephesians 6:12-14). Steadfastly hold your ground. Don't waver. For as James 1:6-8 says, "...*He that wavers is like a wave of the sea driven with the wind and tossed.... Let not that man think that he shall receive anything of the Lord. A double minded man is unstable in all his ways."*

Above all, keep your attention trained on the Word—not on lingering symptoms. Be like Abraham who *"considered not his own body"* (Romans 4:19). Instead of focusing on your circumstances, focus on what God has said to you.

Develop an inner image of yourself with your healing fully manifested. See yourself well. See yourself whole. See yourself healed in every way.

Since what you keep before your eyes and in your ears determines what you will believe in your heart and what you will act on, make the Word your number one priority. Keep taking God's medicine as directed and trust the Great Physician to do His wonderful healing work in you!

What to Do When Healing Doesn't Manifest

You know God wants you healed, and you have taken all the steps you know from God's Word to receive your healing. But for some reason, your circumstances just do not seem to be changing... healing is not manifesting in your body.

What do you do now?

First, it is important to understand that God has not failed you. He cannot, because there is no failure in Him. It is never God who is short on healing power. Healing always comes. However, it is not always received.

When demands are made on the power of God, the healing virtue of Jesus Christ will flow into a person's body and make it whole.

In John 5, the story is told about a man who had an infirmity for 38 years. This story, perhaps, gives us the best picture of the frustration that even today's believers face when it comes to wanting to be healed, and yet, not being able to *make it happen* when we want it—and need it—the most.

We read that day after day the invalid man lay by the pool of Bethesda hoping somehow to be the first person in the water after the angel stirred it, because if he was the first to make it in, he could be healed.

But then along came Jesus. He asked the man, "Do you want to become well?" The invalid answered saying, "Sir, I have nobody when the water is moving to put me into the pool...." (See verses 6-7, *The Amplified Bible*.)

The significant detail in their conversation at this point is that the man was so focused on the problem of not being able to get into the water before someone else, that he never even considered placing a demand on Jesus to help him—to get him healed.

Like this man, many believers today desire to be healed, yet they have not willed to be healed. What's the difference?

The difference is that *determination* is what makes a demand on the power of God. After all, God has sent His Word, and according to that Word, healing has already been purchased by the blood of Jesus. So, the rest is up to us. We must act on this new blood covenant to get the results we desire.

Still, for those times when it seems God's healing power has somehow been short-circuited and it just is not flowing through our lives, the Bible points out some problem areas that may be the reason for this lack of healing or health. Some of those problem areas include:

> Failure to forgive others (Mark 11:25-26)
> Failure to keep the commandment of love (John 13:34)
> Lack of knowledge and lack of vision (Hosea 4:6; Proverbs 29:18)
> Lack of discernment of the Lord's body when taking communion (I Corinthians 11:23-32)
> Lack of integrity in your heart (Psalms 25:21)

Since we know there is no failure with God, it is obvious that when believers do not receive their healing, the problem must lie elsewhere. Keeping this in mind, we need to realize that healing largely depends on a firm stand in the fact that your prayer has been heard, and, that it *has been* answered.

The challenge, then, comes in not swaying from God's Word. And in part, that means we need to keep our tongue in line with what God says about our healing.

To help you stay in line with the *final Word* on healing, we suggest you take the following scriptures, look them up in your Bible, then read them over and over, and meditate on them. It may even help you to write or type them out on separate paper so you can have easier access to them throughout your day.

Proverbs 10:11; 12:18; 13:3; 15:4; 16:24; 18:21

Psalms 34:13-14; I Peter 3:10-11

By the way, you may find it interesting to know that nine of the 11 plagues that came against Israel, as recorded in the book of Numbers, were caused by misuse of the tongue. So you see, your mouth—and your words—will either work for you, and bring health and healing to your life, or they will work against you, bringing nothing but harm.

Make your words work for your good. Make them get on track with what God has said and is saying.

Speak the Word—and keep speaking it and keep speaking it. As you do, God will confirm it. And He says, *"you are healed!"*

Reference Scriptures that define and demonstrate the words, confess, profess, declare, foretell, proclaim, and prophesy.

Romans 10:9-10, Hebrews 10:23; Mark 5; Mark 11:23-24; Mark 9:23; Psalm 35:27;

1John 5:4; 1Timothy 6:12-13; James 1:22; Hebrews 3:1; Hebrews 4:14; Matthew 4:4

Chapter 8

STEPPING INTO GOD'S GLORY

everal times in my life I have experienced God's healing power. It has been so marvelous when God has lifted me out of financial difficulties and supplied my needs supernaturally. And what a thrill is has been to stand in faith on God's promises—stepping out of trouble and into victory!

If you know what that's like, you're probably saying, "Oh, yes! Amen. That's the greatest way to live!"

But fasten your spiritual seat belt, my friend. God has shown me in His Word that He has something even better for us. It's a life so powerful, it exceeds anything we could ever ask or think—a life so full of the fiery light of God that darkness of every kind flees from its very presence.

There are some religious folks who will never think we should ever expect anything grand and glorious in this world—just in the world to come. They try to keep people from getting their hopes up.

On the contrary: My best intention is to get your hopes up. When I say "hope," I'm not talking about the weak, wistful kind of wishing the world calls *hope*. I'm talking about real, Bible hope, the kind of hope the Apostle Paul was referring to when he said: *"For I know that this shall turn to my salvation through your prayer, and the supply of the Spirit of Jesus Christ [the Anointed of God], according to my earnest expectation and my hope, that in nothing I shall be ashamed..."* (Philippians 1:19-20).

The terms "earnest expectation" and "hope" found in that scripture come from two Greek words, each of which can be accurately translated hope. Paul put both of them side by side for emphasis.

If you'll research the term, hope—you'll find it means a confident expectation, a happy anticipation of good, a strained expectancy and eager longing. They refer to an expectation so strong that it absorbs all your attention.

Raise Your Expectation

If you know how to live by faith, you've experienced that kind of hope. Maybe you've been sick, for example, and you set your hope on the fact that by the stripes of Jesus, you were healed (I Peter 2:24).

You began to meditate on those scriptures until you built an inner image of yourself healed. As that image grew more crisp and clear, you began to expect—or hope for—that image to become reality. Eventually, faith rose up, put substance to that internal image and turned it into a manifested reality.

What you did was activate God's Word described in Hebrews 11:1: *"Faith is the substance of things hoped for...."* That spiritual process always works the same way. Hope forms the image according to the Word, then faith rises up and gives substance to that image, making it a reality in the natural, physical realm.

So, in the light of all God has promised us in His Word, what are you and I to expect? What should we be hoping for? What inner image should so capture our hearts and minds that it is all we can see?

Certainly, healing is great. Financial supply is also great. But could it be that God has something even grander for us to fix our hope upon?

Yes, He does according to Romans 5:1-2: *"Therefore being justified by faith, we have peace with God through our Lord Jesus Christ [the Anointed One]: By whom also we have access by faith into this grace wherein we stand, and rejoice in hope of the glory of God."*

Read that last phrase again. It says we're to rejoice in the hope of the glory of God! We're to expect the glory of God, not just the healing!

As long as you just expect healing, you'll always be battling it out with your flesh. But if you expect the glory, you'll be raising your spiritual sights to something bigger than healing. You'll be expecting the very presence of God to rise up in you so powerfully that instead of believing for healing every six weeks, you'll walk in divine health every day!

When you expect the glory, you'll start living like what you really are—joint heirs with Jesus!

> *"The glory which You gave Me I have given them,*
> *that they may be one just as We are one."*
>
> John 17:22

What Is *God's Glory?*

When God's glory is mentioned in the book of Genesis, it's referring to the wealth of God. So, God's glory includes His wealth, but it's much, much more than that. The word *glory* actually means "heavyweight." God is *heavy* with everything you could ever want or need. He is so heavy with healing that if everyone in the whole world believed Him for healing at once, no one would have to wait until tomorrow to get healed because God got tired.

In the book of Exodus, God's glory could be seen going before the Israelites in a pillar of a cloud by day and in a pillar of fire by night (Exodus 13:21). Habakkuk described God's glory as lightning-like shafts of splendor that streamed from His hands. "...and there [in the sunlike splendor] was the hiding place of His power" (Habakkuk 3:4, *The Amplified Bible*). And when Ezekiel saw God in His glory, he said He was a fire from the loins up and from the loins down (Ezekiel 8:2).

The *fire* of God is called the glory. The *wind* of God is called the glory. The *smoke* of God is called the glory. The *fullness* of God is called the glory. It is *all* the glory because the glory of God refers to the supernatural life and essence of God. The very power that makes Him God!

Many have thought that kind of awesome glory must be reserved for God and God alone. Not according to the Bible. Psalms 8:5 tells us that in the beginning man was crowned with that glory—crowned with the same fire and flame of beauty that was on God Himself.

To crown means to anoint! God put His hands on their heads and crowned them with His own presence and glory so that they began to shine just like He shines. They were not standing unclothed and vulnerable to the elements but surrounded and protected by a shimmering force field of glory.

That glory was lost to mankind when Adam sinned. But what most believers don't realize is that the glory was restored when Jesus was resurrected! Romans 6:4 says not only that "Christ was raised up from the dead by the glory of the Father" but also "even so [or by that same glory] we also should walk in newness of life."

You and I are supposed to be walking in the glory! We get a glimpse of what that's like in the Bible account of the glory flowing out of the Apostle Peter with such force that people were healed as he walked by them: "Insomuch that they brought forth the sick into the streets, and laid them on beds and couches, that at the least the shadow of Peter passing by might overshadow some of them" (Acts 5:15). It wasn't Peter's shadow that healed them but that field of glory that surrounded him.

That's what God put hope in you to expect. *The glory!* Not just healing. Not just increase of finances. Not just deliverance. All those things are great and they're all available to us, but God wants us to raise our expectations higher than that. He wants us to expect the glory! Everything we could ever need, and more than we would ever want, can be found in the glory of God!

It's a Mystery

Where is God's glory? Not off in heaven somewhere, waiting for some great prophet of faith to pull it down. Not hovering out there behind heaven's gates. It is inside you!

I can almost hear your mind working: *I just can't understand how that can be!*

I know you can't. It's a mystery! As the Apostle Paul said in Colossians 1:26-27:

> *"Even the mystery which hath been hid from ages*
> *and from generations, but now is made manifest to*

*his saints: To whom God would make known what
is the riches of the glory of this mystery among the
Gentiles; which is Christ [or the Anointing] in you,
the hope of glory."*

Do you realize what that verse is saying? It's saying that the
anointing of Jesus Himself, the very glory of God that raised Him
from the dead, is residing right now within you and every other
believer on the face of this earth. II Corinthians 4 confirms that
fact, saying:

*For God, who commanded the light to shine out of
darkness, hath shined in our hearts, to give the light
of the knowledge of the glory of God in the face of
Jesus Christ. But we have this treasure [what treasure? the glory of God!] in earthen vessels, that the
excellency of the power may be of God, and not of
us.... For we which live are always delivered unto
death for Jesus' sake, that the life also of Jesus might
be made manifest in our mortal flesh (verses 6-7, 11).*

The glory of God is in you! The faith of God is in you. The love
of God is in you. The mind of Christ, the Anointed One, is in you.
All the fruit of the spirit is in you. Healing is in you. Deliverance is
in you. All the wealth of heaven itself is in you. Those things were
born in you when you were born again and they ought to be flowing
out of that mortal, subject-to-death, meat-and-blood-and-bone body
you're living in right now! The glory of God should be pouring out
of that earthen vessel!

Why isn't it? Because we've never developed the expectancy for it.

We've had the idea that glory will only come when God decides
*Boy, I'm going to show them something today. They haven't seen
My glory for 2,000 years.* Then, Pow! He just shoots the earth with
some big glory gun!

No! The glory of God is within us! It is going to manifest when
we meditate on the glory of God so much that hope rises up and

provides an image. Then faith will release the glory of God from the inside of us where we *can't* see it—to the outside where we can see it!

Remember the words Jesus spoke to Martha when Lazarus died? He told her, *"Said I not unto thee, that, if thou wouldest believe, thou shouldest see the glory of God?"* (John 11:40).

Those words are just as true for us as they were for Martha. If we'll believe for the glory, if we'll meditate on the Word of God until we develop our hope and begin to intensely expect the glory, then faith will become the substance of it—and we'll begin to see it.

Does that sound wild to you? Well, it's not!

If you'll go back and read the Bible, you'll see that's what Christianity is all about. God intended for the Body of Christ to walk through this earth with such a manifestation of His presence in our lives that it would either scare people spitless...or draw them into the kingdom of God!

The Apostle Paul, knowing God intended us to have a foretaste of the resurrected body right here on the earth, wrote:

> *"[For my determined purpose is] that I may know Him...and that I may in that same way come to know the power outflowing from His resurrection...that if possible I may attain to the...resurrection [that lifts me] out from among the dead [even while in the body]"*
> Philippians 3:10-11, *The Amplified Bible*.

I've experienced little touches of that kind of glory and, believe me, I'm eager for more. *More* is coming, too!

Ashes Under Our Feet

Malachi 4:2-3 promises:

> *"But unto you that fear my name shall the Sun of righteousness arise with healing in his wings; and ye shall go forth, and grow up as calves of the stall.*

*And ye shall tread down the wicked; for they shall
be ashes under the soles of your feet in the day that I
shall do this, saith the Lord of hosts."*

Notice that scripture said "Sun of righteousness" not "Son of
righteousness." It's talking about a bright, blazing glory. And the
wings it refers to aren't birds' wings, they're flames of fire that are
shaped like wings.

But most exciting of all is the fact that Malachi didn't say that
"*He* shall go forth." He said, "[*You*] shall go forth." You and I are
the ones who are going to go forth with this blazing glory—the same
glory that appeared as a pillar of fire by night and cloud by day...
the same glory that filled the temple with such power the priests
couldn't approach the altar without being knocked backward...the
same glory that raised Jesus from the dead...the same glory that God
said would fill the whole earth—that same glory is what we'll use to
tread down the devil until he is ashes under our feet!

The expectancy of that glory is going to grow so strong between
now and Jesus' return that it is going to fill churches. It's going to
come on congregations with such power that people are going to run
from all over the neighborhood to find out what it is.

The glory is coming! Your confession of faith and your expectancy are going to pull it out of you, and you're going to walk in that
glory right in the face of hell and everything it has to offer.

Dare to release your expectancy of the glory. Before long you'll
realize...*you haven't seen anything yet!*

JEREMIAH 31:33

This is the covenant that I will make with the house of Israel after those days, says the Lord: I will put My law in their minds, and write it on their hearts; and I will be their God, and they shall be My people.

Chapter 9

FAITH FOR MIRACLES

M̲ost people (and most Christians) don't know how to "live" in God's supernatural secret place. Why? Because most people cannot look beyond the physical circumstances. Many people cannot see with "eyes of faith." Sometimes when we have a revelation of God's awesome promises, most of the people around us cannot understand.

> *"Now faith is the substance of things hoped for, the evidence of things not seen."*
>
> Hebrews 11:1

Can You Hear Me Now?

One of my favorite stories about knowing a secret that no one else knows is from the Great Depression here in the United States. An employer let the word out that he had a job opening, and immediately a long line of applicants formed outside his office. His secretary showed the applicants into the bosses office one at a time.

All of a sudden, one man ran from the back of the line, passed the secretary, and right into the bosses office. After just a short time, the boss came out wit the man and announced that everyone else could go home. Many were complaining and grumbling that it was unfair that this man had not waited his turn.

The boss explained that during the interview process, he thought of a quicker way to select the best person for the job. He needed someone who could understand Morse Code, so he "tapped out" so that everyone could hear, "If you can hear this, jump up now and run to my office. You have the job."

All the men and women in line heard the tapping, but it did not mean anything to them; however, it changed the life of this new employee.

Can you see how the Lord God has been teaching us His secret ways? Unbelievers can not, because they will not, tap into God's way of worship, prayer, meditating His Word, and speaking the Word. The Lord God has selected things that seem foolish to those who are prideful, carnally minded, self-centered, and self sufficient.

Faith – Anchored in the Unseen

Faith is the mirror of the heart that reflects the realities of an unseen world—the actual substance of God's Kingdom.

Through the prayer of faith we are able to pull the reality of His world into this one. That is the function of faith.

Faith has its anchor in the unseen realm. It lives from the invisible toward the visible. Faith actualizes what it realizes. The Scriptures contrast the life of faith with the limitations of natural sight. Faith provides eyes for the heart.

Jesus expects people to see from the heart. He once called a group of religious leaders hypocrites because they could discern the weather but couldn't discern the times. It's obvious why Jesus would prefer people to recognize the times (spiritual climate and seasons) over natural weather conditions, but it's not quite so apparent why He would consider them hypocrites if they didn't.

Many of us have thought that the ability to see into the spiritual realm is more the result of a special gift than an unused potential of everyone. I remind you that Jesus addresses this charge to the Pharisees and Sadducees. The very fact that they, of all people, were required to see is evidence that everyone has been given this ability. They became blind to His dominion because of their own corrupted hearts and were judged for their unfulfilled potential.

We are born again by grace through faith. The born again experience enables us to see from the heart. A heart that doesn't see is a hard heart. Faith was never intended only to get us into the family. Rather, it is the nature of life in this family. Faith sees. It brings

His Kingdom into focus. All of the Father's resources, all of His benefits, are accessible through faith.

To encourage us in our capacity to see, Jesus gave specific instruction, *"Seek first the kingdom of God...."* Paul taught us, *"Set your mind on things above, not on things on the earth."* He also stated, "For the things which are seen are temporary, but the things which are not seen are eternal." The Bible instructs us to turn our attention toward the invisible. This theme is repeated enough in Scripture to make those of us bound by the logic of this Western culture quite nervous.

Herein lies the secret to the supernatural realm that we want restored to the Church. Jesus told us that He only did what He saw His Father do. Such an insight is vital for those who want more. The power of His actions, for instance, the mud in the eye of the blind, is rooted in His ability to see.

Worship and the Power of Faith

God is very committed to teaching us how to see. To make this possible He gave us the Holy Spirit as a teacher. The curriculum that He uses is quite varied. But the one class we all qualify for is the greatest of all Christian privileges—worship. Learning how to see is not the purpose for our worship, but it is a wonderful by-product.

Those who worship in spirit and truth, as mentioned in John 4:23-24, learn to follow the Holy Spirit's lead. His realm is called the kingdom of God. The throne of God, which becomes established upon the praises of His people, is the center of that Kingdom. It's in the environment of worship that we learn things that go way beyond what our intellect can grasp—and the greatest of these lessons is the value of His Presence. David was so affected by this that all his other exploits pale in comparison to his abandoned heart for God. We know that he learned to see into God's realm because of statements like, "I have set the Lord always before me; because He is at my right hand I shall not be moved."

The Presence of God affected his seeing. He would constantly practice recognizing the Presence of God. He saw God daily, not with the natural eyes, but with the eyes of faith. That priceless revelation was given to a worshiper.

The privilege of worship is a good beginning place for those unaccustomed to addressing some of these kinds of themes found in Scripture. It's in that wonderful ministry that we can learn to pay attention to this God-given gift: the ability to see with the heart. As we learn to worship with purity of heart, our eyes will continue to open. And we can expect to see what He wants us to see.

Seeing the Invisible

The invisible realm is superior to the natural. The reality of that invisible world dominates the natural world we live in...both positively and negatively. Because the invisible is superior to the natural, faith is anchored in the unseen.

Faith lives within the revealed will of God. When I have misconceptions of who He is and what He is like, my faith is restricted by those misconceptions. For example, if I believe that God allows sickness in order to build character, I'll not have confidence praying in most situations where healing is needed. But, if I believe that sickness is to the body what sin is to the soul, then no disease will intimidate me. Faith is far more free to develop when we truly see the heart of God as good.

The same misconceptions of God affect those who need to have faith for their own miracle. A woman who needed a miracle once told me that she felt God had allowed her sickness for a purpose. I told her that if I treated my children that way I'd be arrested for child abuse. She agreed and eventually allowed me to pray for her. After truth came into her heart, her healing came minutes later.

Unbelief is anchored in what is visible or reasonable apart from God. It honors the natural realm as superior to the invisible. The apostle Paul states that what you can see is temporal, and what you can't see is eternal. Unbelief is faith in the inferior.

The natural realm is the anchor of unbelief. But that realm is not to be considered as evil. Rather the humble of heart recognize the hand of God through what is seen. God has created all things to speak of Him—whether it is rivers and trees, or angels and heaven.

The natural realm carries the witness of His greatness...for those with eyes to see and ears to hear.

Realist or Materialist

Most all of the people that I've known who are filled with unbelief have called themselves realists. This is an honest evaluation, but not one to be proud of. Those kinds of realists believe more in what is visible than they do in what they can't see. Put another way, they believe the material world rules over the spiritual world.

Materialism has been thought simply to be the accumulation of goods. Although it includes that, it is much more. I can own nothing and still be materialistic. I can want nothing and be materialistic because materialism is faith in the natural as the superior reality.

We are a sensual society with a culture shaped by what is picked up through the senses. We're trained to believe only in what we see. Real faith is not living in denial of the natural realm. If the doctor says you have a tumor, it's silly to pretend that it's not there. That's not faith. However, faith is founded on a reality that is superior to that tumor. I can acknowledge the existence of a tumor and still have faith in the provision of His stripes for my healing...I was provisionally healed 2,000 years ago. It is the product of the kingdom of heaven—a superior reality. There are no tumors in heaven, and faith brings that reality into this one.

Would Satan like to inflict heaven with cancer? Of course he would. But he has no dominion there. He only has dominion here when and where man has come into agreement.

Living in Denial

Fear of appearing to live in denial is what keeps many from faith. Why is what anyone thinks so important to you that you'd not be willing to risk all to trust God? The fear of man is very strongly associated with unbelief. Conversely, the fear of God and faith are very closely related.

People of faith are also realists. They just have their foundation in a superior reality.

Unbelief is actually faith in something other than God. He is jealous over our hearts. The one whose primary trust is in another grieves the Holy Spirit.

It's Not in the Head

Faith is born of the Spirit in the hearts of mankind. Faith is neither intellectual nor anti-intellectual. It is superior to the intellect. The Bible does not say, with the mind man believes! Through faith, man is able to come into agreement with the mind of God.

When we submit the things of God to the mind of man, unbelief and religion are the results. When we submit the mind of man to the things of God, we end up with faith and a renewed mind. The mind makes a wonderful servant, but a terrible master.

Much of the opposition to revival comes from soul-driven Christians. The apostle Paul calls them carnal. They have not learned how to be led by the Spirit. Anything that doesn't make sense to their rational mind is automatically in conflict with Scripture. This way of thinking is accepted all throughout the Church in Western civilization, which should explain why our God so often looks just like us.

Most of the goals of the modern church can be accomplished without God. All we need is people, money, and a common objective. Determination can achieve great things. But success is not necessarily a sign that the goal was from God. Little exists in church life to ensure that we are being directed and empowered by the Holy Spirit. Returning to the ministry of Jesus is the only insurance we have of accomplishing such a goal.

Faith From a Relationship

The Holy Spirit lives in my spirit. That is the place of communion with God. As we learn to receive from our spirits we learn how to be Spirit led.

"By faith, we understand." Faith is the foundation for all true wisdom. When we learn to learn that way, we open ourselves up to grow in true faith because faith does not require understanding to function.

I'm sure that most of you have had this experience—you've been reading the Bible, and a verse jumps out at you. There is great excitement over this verse that seems to give so much life and encouragement to you. Yet initially you couldn't teach or explain that verse if your life depended on it.

What happened is this: Your spirit received the life-giving power of the word from the Holy Spirit. When we learn to receive from our spirit, our mind becomes the student and is therefore subject to the Holy Spirit. Through the process of revelation and experience our mind eventually obtains understanding. That is biblical learning— the spirit giving influence to the mind.

Faith is Both Substance and Evidence

"Now faith is the substance of things hoped for, the evidence of things not seen." (Hebrews 11:1.)

Faith is the mirror of the heart that reflects the realities of His world into ours. It is the substance of the unseen realm. This wonderful gift from God is the initial earthly manifestation of what exists in His Kingdom. It is a testimony of an invisible realm called the Kingdom of God. Through prayer we are able to pull that reality into this one—that is how faith functions.

If I go into the local pizza parlor and order a pizza, they will give me a number and a receipt. I am to place that number in a conspicuous place on the table. Someone may walk in off the street and come to my table and announce that they won't give me any pizza. I'll just point to the number and tell him, When pizza number 52 is done, it's mine! That number is the substance of the pizza hoped for. If that guy tells me that my number isn't any good, I'll point to my receipt. It verifies the value of the number. When my pizza is done, the waiter will walk around looking for my number. How does the product of heaven know where to land? He looks for the substance...the number. If a question comes up over the validity of my number, my receipt, which is contained in the Bible, verifies my right to both the number and the pizza.

Heaven is not moved simply by the needs of man. It's not that God doesn't care. It was out of His great compassion that He sent Jesus. When God is moved by human need He seldom fixes the problem outright; instead, He provides Kingdom principles that when embraced correct the problems. If God was moved solely by human need then countries like India and Haiti would become the wealthiest nations in the world. It doesn't work like that. Heaven is moved by faith. Faith is the currency of heaven.

The Source of Faith

"Faith comes by hearing...." It does not say that it comes from having heard. It is the listening heart, in the present tense, that is ready for heaven's deposit of faith. Abraham heard God tell him to sacrifice his son Isaac. When he drew back the sword to slay his son the Lord spoke again. This time He told Abraham that the test was over and that he passed—he was not to sacrifice his son. Had he only done what God had said he would have killed his son. Hearing now — is a key to faith.

The apostle Paul was driven by the command, *"Go into all the world and preach the gospel...."* However, when he was ready to preach the gospel in Asia, God said no. What God had said appeared to be in conflict with what God was saying. Paul then prepared to go to Bithynia. Again, God said no. Following this Paul had a dream of a man calling out to him from Macedonia. This was recognized as the will of God, and they went.

Even though we may know the will of God from Scripture, we still need the Holy Spirit to help us with the interpretation, application, and empowerment to perform His will.

Fearfulness

The biblical command repeated most often is: Do not fear. Why? Fear attacks the foundation of our relationship with God...our faith. Fear is faith in the devil; it is also called unbelief. Jesus would ask His fearful disciples, "Why are you so faithless?" because fearfulness is the same as faithlessness. Fear and faith cannot coexist—they work against each other.

The devil is called Beelzebub, which means, lord of the flies. He and his hosts are attracted to decay.

Issues such as bitterness, jealousy, and hatred qualify as the decay of the heart that invites the devil to come and give influence—yes, even to Christians. Remember Paul's admonition to the church of Ephesus, "Neither give place to the devil." Fear is also a decay of the heart. It attracts the demonic in the same way as bitterness and hatred. How did the flies know where my freezer was? Through the scent of decaying meat. Fear gives off a similar scent. Like faith, fear is substance in the spiritual realm. Satan has no power except through our agreement. Fear becomes our heart's response when we come into agreement with his intimidating suggestions.

React or Respond

Many who have feared the excesses made by others in the name of faith have ironically embraced unbelief. Reaction to error usually produces error.

On the other hand, response to truth always wins out over those who react to error. Some people would have no belief system were it not for the error of others. Fortunately, their thoughts and teachings become the opposite of what others believe and practice.

It is also true that those who strive for balance become weak. The word balance has come to mean middle of the road—of no threat to people or the devil, with little risk, and above all...the best way to keep our nice image intact.

The Church warns its members about the great sin of presumption. God warns us of the sin of unbelief. Jesus didn't say, When I return will I find people who are excessive and presumptuous? He wanted to find people with faith, the very kind He displayed. While we often huddle in groups of like-minded people, those with faith blaze a trail that threatens all of our comfort zones. Faith offends the stationary.

People of great faith are hard to live with. Their reasoning is out of this world. I have read about great men and women of God of the early 1900s. I've learned that not everyone liked Smith

Wigglesworth. His strong faith made other people feel uncomfortable. We either become like them or we avoid them. We find their lifestyle either contagious or offensive with little neutral ground. Smith is well loved today...but it's only because he's dead. Israel loved their dead prophets too.

There's something amazing about unbelief—it is able to fulfill its own expectations. Unbelief is safe because it takes no risk and almost always gets what it expects. Then, after a person gets the answer for their unbelief, they can say, I told you so.

Chapter 10

A HIGHER REALITY

F aith is not just an abiding faith; it's active. It's aggressive by nature. It has focus and purpose. Faith grabs hold of the reality of the Kingdom and forcefully and aggressively brings it into a collision with this natural world.

One of the more common things people tell me when I'm about to pray for their healing is, "I know God can do it." But the truth is that even the devil knows it. At best that is hope...not faith. Faith "knows" He will.

For one who has faith, there is nothing impossible. There are no impossibilities when there is faith...and there are no exceptions.

Ears to Hear

"So then faith comes by hearing, and hearing by the word of God." Notice it does not say, faith comes from having heard. The whole nature of faith implies a relationship with God that is current. The emphasis is on hearing...in the now!

In the book of Genesis, God told Abraham to sacrifice Isaac. As Abraham raised the knife to slay his son, God spoke again. This time He told him not to slay his son, as he had passed the test of being willing to do anything for God. It's a good thing that Abraham's only connection with God was not just over what was already said, but was based upon what He was "saying!"

What this world needs is for the Church to return to a show and tell message on the kingdom of God. They need an anchor that is greater than everything they can see. The world system has no answers to the world's increasing problems—every solution is only temporary.

Faith is not the absence of doubt; it's the presence of belief. I may not always feel that I have great faith. But I can always obey, laying my hands on someone and praying. It's a mistake for me to ever examine my faith. I seldom find it. It's better for me to obey quickly. After it's over I can look back and see that my obedience came from faith.

The Transformation Effect

When an assembly of believers grow stronger in faith, it has a transformation effect, where innocent bystanders get touched by the miracle-working power of God.

Transformational faith pulls on heaven in marvelous ways. God's world becomes manifest all around us.

Just as fear is a tangible element in the spirit world, so faith is tangible there. In the natural a loud voice may intimidate another man. But devils know the difference between the one who is truly bold and aggressive because of their faith, and the one who is simply covering his fears with aggressive behavior. Christians often use this tactic when casting out devils. Many of us have yelled threats, called on angels for help, promised to make it harder on the demons on Judgment Day, and other foolish things only to try and cover immature fear. Real faith is anchored in the invisible realm and is connected to the authority given in the name of the Lord Jesus Christ.

The authority to cast out demons is found in rest. Rest is the climate that faith grows in. It comes out of the peace of God. And it is the Prince of Peace who will soon crush Satan underneath our feet! What is restful for us is violent to the powers of hell. That is the violent nature of faith.

This is not to be a soulish attempt at self-confidence or self-determination. Instead it is a moving of the heart into a place of surrender...a place of rest. A surrendered heart is a heart of faith. And faith must be present to please God.

The Force of Faith

> *"Until now the kingdom of heaven suffers violence,*
> *and the violent take it by force."*
>
> Matthew 11:12.

I believe the key to this verse is to understand the word "violence." The Greek word for violence is "BIAZO." This word is also found in Luke 16:16 — and means "pressing in." Before the time of John the Baptist, the only way to approach God was through the Old Testament laws and sacrifices. (People of that day could be described as passive and merely "going through the motions.")

When John came preaching by the power of the Spirit, people began to truly "press in" to the kingdom of heaven — overcoming any obstacle or opposition posed by laws, traditions, unbelief, or any power Satan threw at them, in order to receive the Good News message. They were "violently resolved" in their zeal and forcefully pressing in to the kingdom of heaven.

Today, Satan is still opposing the preaching of the Gospel, and only those who are seriously pressing in to receive God's best will have it. (James 4:7; 1 John 5:4.)

Here's an example: Two blind men who sat by the road called out to Jesus. People told them to be quiet. That only hardened their determination. They became more desperate and cried out all the louder. He called them forth and healed them saying, "The kingdom has come near you." He attributed their miracle to their faith.

A woman who had a blood disorder for 12 years pressed through a crowd. When she was finally able to touch the garment of Jesus, she was healed. He attributed it to her faith.

The stories of this kind are many, all with similar endings—they were healed or delivered because of their faith. Faith may quietly press in, or it may cry out very loudly, but it is always violent in the spirit world. It grabs hold of an invisible reality and won't let go. Taking the Kingdom by faith is the violent act that is necessary to come into what God has made available.

Faith Empowers

An automobile may have several hundred horsepower. But the car will go nowhere until the clutch is released, connecting the power contained in the running motor and transferring that power to the wheels. So it is with faith. We have all the power of heaven behind us. But it is our faith that connects to that power. Faith takes what is available and makes it active.

It's not wrong to try to grow in faith. It's not wrong to seek for signs and the increase of miracles. Those are all within the rights of the believer. But learning how to pray is the task at hand. It's the only thing the disciples asked Jesus to teach them.

DEUTERONOMY 8:18

You shall remember the LORD your God, for it is He who gives you power to get wealth, that He may establish His covenant which He swore to your fathers, as it is this day.

Chapter 11

IN CHRIST JESUS NOW!

D o you know who you are? I'm not talking about who you are because of your parents, your background, or your upbringing, or because of someone who led you into sin. I mean, do you really know who you are "in Christ?"

Most people know who they are in the natural realm as it relates to their family and upbringing, but when it comes to their true identity in Christ and what that entails, they don't have a clue.

Often, people have a hard time identifying with God because they relate to their own physical, natural identities and the things they can perceive with their senses more than they do with Him.

God made us in His image, and when we accept Jesus as our Lord and personal Savior, we become one with Him. This means that, from a spiritual perspective, we are just like Him; in the spirit. Knowing who we are in Christ is the catalyst for walking in the power of God and demonstrating that power to the world.

Because the knowledge of who we are in Christ is so vital to our confidence as sons of God, it is the area in which Satan will consistently attack us.

In fact, he attacked Jesus in the area of identity when He was fasting in the wilderness for forty days and forty nights.

> *"when He had fasted forty days and forty nights, afterward He was hungry. Now when the tempter came to Him, he said, "If You are the Son of God, command that these stones become bread."*
>
> Matthew 4:2-3

When Satan tried to question Jesus' identity in the wilderness, Jesus responded with the Word of God. He didn't have to prove anything because He knew who He was! That is the same way we should respond to the devil when He comes to attack our identity in Christ. We should always remind Him of what God has said about us and about him. Jesus said to him, "It is written again, *'You shall not tempt the LORD your God"* (v. 7). When Satan realized that Jesus was not moved by His attack, and that He knew who He was, the Bible says he left Him alone.

Jesus wasn't the first one Satan attacked in the area of identity. In the Garden of Eden, he also attacked Adam and Eve. He made a statement that suggested to them that they weren't who God had made them to be. In Genesis 3:1-5, Satan deceived Eve into thinking that she wasn't like God, which was the opposite of the truth. God had created Adam and Eve in His image, which meant that they already were like Him. They allowed the voice of the enemy to get them to doubt who they really were. As a result, they took the bait and fell into his trap.

By constantly looking into the mirror of God's Word, we are able to maintain a consistent consciousness of our identity in Christ.

The Word will tell us exactly who we are, what we look like from God's perspective, and how we are to act as sons of God. It will also reveal to us any areas of our lives that may not line up with God's Word.

God is a spiritual being, and He has made us in His image. When we become born again, we carry the very nature of God on the inside of us, which makes "like Him," or joined together as extensions of Himself; (Psalm 82:1-8, AMP).

Therefore, we should identify with the identity that God has given us. Philippians 2:5-9 shows us the attitude we should have as Believers:

> *"Let this mind be in you, which was also in Christ Jesus: Who, being in the form of God, thought it not robbery to be equal with God: But made himself of no reputation, and took upon him the form of a servant, and was made in the likeness of men: And*

*being found in fashion as a man, he humbled himself,
and became obedient unto death, even the death of
the cross."*

Even though we possess the power of God on the inside of us,
if we don't embrace the same mind-set that Jesus had about His
identity, for our own lives, we'll never be confident enough to walk
in that identity.

From now on, begin to see yourself as Jesus saw Himself—a
spiritual being who possessed everything that the Father God has
freely given. Renew your mind to who you really are and declare it
every day. You will send the devil running in the opposite direction!

Receiving a New Identity

Did you know that if you are born again, you are part of a royal
family? It doesn't matter what your background is, the color of your
skin, or which side of the tracks you grew up on. Jesus has leveled
the playing field for each and every person who chooses to accept
Him as Lord and Savior.

When we become followers of Christ, something supernatural
takes place in our spirits; we are re-created spiritually and have
access to everything heaven has to offer. Our job is to renew our
minds to the new identity we have received through Christ.

Many Christians are going through an identity crisis because
they simply don't know who they are and what they have access to
as a result of their relationship with Jesus.

The Bible is a book of promises, or covenants, between God and
His people. All He wants us to do is believe His Word and lay hold
of the good things He has for us, by faith. We have to know we have
a right to these things, however, because of who we are in Christ.

*"Therefore if any man be in Christ, he is a new crea-
ture: old things are passed away; behold, all things
are become new."*

Second Corinthians 5:17

When we accept Jesus, our spirits are literally recreated; we are not who we used to be, from a spiritual perspective. After the salvation experience, we must enter into the process of renewing our minds so our thinking will begin to line up with the conversion we have experienced.

As our thoughts about ourselves change through continual study and application of God's Word, we will begin to see ourselves differently, and consequently, we will begin to act differently. The things we used to do, we just won't be able to do any more.

As Believers, we have been changed into another spiritual species that is no longer connected to the world system and the laws that govern it. Our new identity is in Christ, and just like a king on earth, we are seated in a spiritual position with Him that surpasses the forces of darkness (Ephesians 2:6).

We have access to the very nature of God, and all of His promises (2 Peter 1:3, 4). In order to align our lives with this new identity, we must renew our minds (Romans 12:1, 2). We must look into the Word of God like we look in the mirror in the morning because the Word will reflect back to us who we really are as born again people. By allowing the Scriptures to transform our thinking about who we are, and declaring what God has said about us, we can begin to experience what abundant living is all about!

Change Your Thinking, Change Your Life

Our thinking sets the course for our lives. If we find we are not living the abundant life Jesus died to give us, we must examine our thought life.

"For as a man thinks in his heart, so is he" (Proverbs 23:7).

In order to prosper God's way, our thoughts must agree with His Word. The words we are exposed to on a daily basis have a huge impact on our thinking. And the condition of our minds determines the condition of our lives.

Therefore, as Believers, we must go through the process of renewing our minds with the Word of God. Then, when we have thoughts that do not line up with God's Word, we can replace them with Word-based thoughts (2 Corinthians 10:5).

It is the will of God for us to prosper in every way, from our health and finances to our relationships and jobs. Every area of our lives should be an expression of abundant life.

However, we prosper to the degree that our souls prosper (3 John 2). The soul is where the mind, will, and emotions reside. The mind is the primary area that Satan attacks because it is the control center of our lives.

Satan's attacks consist of words and images that oppose God's Word. He wants us to doubt God and fear that His promises will never come to pass. However, we have the power to transform our lives. Transformation comes when we allow God's Word to change our thinking.

> *"Do not be conformed to this world, but be trans-formed by the renewing of your mind, that you may prove what is that good and acceptable and perfect will of God."*
>
> Romans 12:2

Many Believers wonder why their lives have not changed since they've been saved. The problem lies within their thinking. Many of us have nourished mindsets that actually "oppose" the Word for years — and as a result, our old nature is stronger than our regenerated spirits.

In order for change to occur, we must begin to nourish godly thoughts by consistently meditating on the Word.

Keep in mind that change does not occur overnight; it is a process during which we must refuse to become frustrated.

When we remain committed to the transformation process, we will begin to see changes takes place. Change is a lifetime endeavor, not a one-time event.

My prayer is that you will continue to conform to the image of Christ by renewing your mind with God's Word on a daily basis, so that you can truly know His good and perfect will for your life.

Powerful Prepositions

One of the most important ways to renew your thinking to "who you are" in Christ Jesus – is to look for all the phrases in the New Testament that include, "in," "through," "by," "with," "on," and "of." Christ Jesus.

You might be surprised to find more than 130 times phrases like, "in Christ," "in Whom," and "in Him."

> *"In Him dwells all the fullness of the Godhead bodily; and you are complete in Him, who is the head of all principality and power"*
>
> Colossians 2:9-10.

Your true identity is not in your past at all. Your true identity is "in Christ Jesus!"

> *"If by the one man's offense death **reign**ed through the one, much more those who receive abundance of grace and of the gift of righteousness will **reign** in life 'through' the One, Jesus Christ"*
>
> Romans 5:17

Even though you are born again, and a member of the Kingdom of Heaven, the devil will do everything he can to keep you from living in the light of who you are in Christ. The key is to "declare continually" who you are in Christ.

Chapter 12

TRUE WORSHIP AND PRAISE

Worship is an essential element of the Christian life and, like praise, is a tool we can use to push the enemy out of our atmosphere. Satan cannot stand to be in the presence of praise, and neither can he stand worship because it brings God's very presence on the scene. Not only that, but it takes the focus off of all his distractions and points our attention completely toward the Lord. Understanding the different ways we can worship gives us a spiritual edge that is vital to a successful relationship with God.

Worship should never be something we do haphazardly or without putting focused intention into it. It is essentially when we express our love, adoration, admiration, and respect for God. We tend to think of worship in terms of the "praise and worship" times we have at church, but as Believers, worship is not limited to the songs we sing before a message is preached from the pulpit. Worship is not entertainment, it's a lifestyle for those who are serious about their relationship with God.

In John 4:23, Jesus says,

> *"But the hour is coming, and now is, when the true worshipers will worship the Father in spirit and truth; for the Father is seeking such to worship Him."*

When we worship God in spirit and in truth, it means we are doing it from our hearts, with a motive of love for God. The Lord knows when something is coming from a place of absolute love and honor in our lives, and it is this type of worship that He desires.

Our obedience to God qualifies as worship because it is in obeying Him that we honor Him. Anything He tells us to do in His Word, and whatever He speaks directly to us to do individually, provides an opportunity for us to worship Him. When we give ourselves over to God completely and are willing to move on even the slightest impulse He gives, our lives actually *become* monuments of worship.

There are at least 5 different ways we can worship God, and all of them require our obedience. Incorporating these things in our daily lives positions us to be the true worshipers the Father is looking for.

1.   Reading and studying the Word.

The study and meditation of God's Word may not fit in the traditional concept of worship, but it is a form of reverence and honor for God. When we focus on the Word of God and internalize it during our study times, it puts us in the spirit, which causes us to embrace the thoughts of God. Our times of study should be special times in which we commune with the Lord and worship Him.

2.   Preaching the Word of God.

What a way to honor and love on God! When we share the Gospel with people and receive the preached Word of God, we are demonstrating our love for God and our obedience to Him.

3.   Singing spiritual songs.

Ephesians 5:18-21 admonishes us to not be drunk with wine, but to be filled with the Spirit of God. It says we are to speak to ourselves in songs, hymns, and spiritual songs, singing and making melody to the Lord in our hearts. This is probably what we consider worship to be, based upon what we experience in church. However, we should incorporate the singing of spiritual songs to the Lord as part of our daily routine. This way, we can keep an atmosphere of worship around us at all times. (1 Corinthians 14:2.)

4.   Prayer and Intercession

Prayer is communication with God, which is also a form of worship. When we intercede for others and stand in the spiritual gap for them, we are also worshiping God through our obedience to Him. We are to always spend time in prayer in order to have a thriving Christian life.

5.   The sacrifice of praise.

Anytime we do something out of obedience and reverence for God, even when our flesh doesn't feel like it, we are worshiping Him. Praise can be a sacrifice because it isn't something we immediately jump to do when times are hard. However, when we do it from our hearts, giving God our best praise, it absolutely paralyzes the enemy and releases God to get involved with the situation.

Worship can be incorporated in every aspect of our daily lives when we make a conscious decision to do so. It is completely abandoning our own wills for the will of God. Becoming a true worshiper will open doors of blessings in our lives and take our relationship with Him to a higher level.

Answers Are Waiting in His Presence

Do you sometimes believe that you can accomplish more on your own, without any help from God? Do you often start your day without even acknowledging His presence? If so, I want to challenge you to begin seeking Him—not just in the morning—but throughout your day. Personally, I take advantage of every opportunity I can to find a quiet place where I can be alone to talk with God, just as I would a close friend. When we cultivate a personal relationship with God, we learn that His way is always better than our own.

Often it seems as if the methods of the world are quicker and easier than God's method; however, I know from experience that His way is always best. Following the world leads to a dead end. However, following God's way leads to a successful, happy life.

Many times, we rush through our days, proceed with our own plans, and place our time with God on the backburner. As a result, we often travel down those dead-end roads. Only when everything else has failed do we call out to him in desperation. Although God doesn't mind showing us mercy during those times, He would rather we seek Him first. Just as a close friend would not want to be chosen as a last resort, God doesn't want to be our last resort either.

When we cultivate a relationship with God, we must understand that He not only wants to be an intricate part of our lives, but He also wants us to delight in the time we spend with Him. When we begin to enjoy spending time with Him, He allows us to know Him on a more intimate level. He reveals mysteries to us when we quiet ourselves and listen more intently for His voice. He will give us answers that only He can give, which will empower us to reach our fullest potential in life.

As we receive His words, we experience a peace that passes all understanding. We begin to have what I call a knowing, deep inside, that He is always there, ready to give us the revelation knowledge we need to operate in power.

In order to reach this secret place, we must keep in mind certain truths that are vital in establishing a relationship with Him. First, we must acknowledge His son, Jesus, who sacrificed His precious blood. I can't emphasize enough the importance of acknowledging the shed blood of Jesus. It is a necessity in the life of a Believer. It is only because of Jesus' sacrifice that we have an opportunity to cultivate a close relationship with the Father.

Also, we must love others unconditionally, because God is love. When we begin to increase our understanding of the love of God and operate in it, we will begin to experience more of Him.

Last but not least, we must learn how to cast our cares on Him, setting aside time each day to clear our minds of clutter. God is always speaking to us, but when our minds are filled with worries and concerns we cannot hear Him!

The answers to the problems you have been struggling with are waiting for you in His presence. I encourage you to begin to seek Him today. Take your relationship with the Lord to a deeper level by giving Him the opportunity to speak into your life—then quickly obey what you hear. Make spending time with Him your new daily habit. And I am confident that you will be so glad you did.

Check Your Hearing

I'm convinced the most valuable asset any Christian has is the ability to hear from God. As a child of God, your success in life depends entirely on your ability to hear the Father's instructions to you and your willingness to obey those instructions.

Hearing from God can mean the difference between life and death. Many Believers come to church every week and pray but still fail to hear from God clearly. Consequently, they continue to make decisions that lead them away from the will of God, instead of making decisions that propel them down God's ordained path for their lives.

Hearing from God is an art that must be cultivated, and it takes practice and diligence to develop this critical part of your relationship with Him. One of the primary keys to hearing from God is having a solid relationship with the Holy Spirit. He dwells in your born-again spirit, and is the guiding force that leads you through life as a Christian (Proverbs 20:27). Only through consistently studying and meditating on God's Word, and fellowshipping with Him through prayer, will you be able to sharpen your ability to hear from Him.

Communication is a vital part of your relationships with others, and it is just as important in your relationship with God. In fact, joint communication is critical. God doesn't just want you to do all the talking; He wants to tell you some things, and give you specific instructions day by day and moment by moment.

How Do I know If I'm hearing from God?

The following guidelines can help you fine-tune your spiritual hearing:

1. Maintain a spirit of expectancy. You must first expect to hear from God, and then expect Him to answer your prayers (Proverbs 23:18; Mark 11:24.).

2. Pray in the spirit (Romans 8:26; Jude 20), pray without ceasing (1 Thessalonians 5:17), and spend time listening for God's voice as you pray.

3. Confirm what you hear with the Word of God (2 Timothy 3:16-17). Everything you hear from God should line up with the Scriptures.
4. Wait for the peace of God (Colossians 3:15).
5. If you have doubts about something you hear, don't move on it.
6. Seek godly counsel (Proverbs 24:6).
7. When you hear something, boldly obey. Every time you obey God, your hearing becomes clearer and more distinct.

In John 10:27, Jesus says, *"My sheep hear my voice, and I know them, and they follow me."* When you make Jesus your Lord and Savior, you gain the ability to hear from God clearly, every day, in specific detail. In fact, the Bible says that not only will you hear His voice, but you will follow Him when He speaks. That is what distinguishes the sheep from the goats; sheep follow their shepherd, while goats do their own thing.

Just like an obedient lamb, you should follow where Jesus leads. It starts by learning to hear from Him and practicing obedience to His written and spoken Word. When you do, you will walk in the perfect will of God for your life.

Praise Your Way to a Breakthrough!

Do you need God to make a way out of no way? The swiftness and surety of your deliverance starts with how you respond to hard times and difficult situations. Hear me when I say that it is not just enough to thank God and honor Him only when you've received a blessing. God wants you to show the extent of your faithfulness and trust in Him even in the midst of going through a challenge. The power of your praise will determine the magnitude of your breakthrough.

Praise is not just clapping your hands or applauding God. It's showing respect, honor, and gratefulness using your whole heart, mind, spirit and body despite your circumstances. Paul and Silas didn't wait until they experienced a breakthrough to praise and thank God. In the midst of difficult circumstances, they praised God and received the breakthrough they desired.

Acts 16:25, 26 (New Living Translation) reveals, *"Around midnight Paul and Silas were praying and singing hymns to God, and the other prisoners were listening. Suddenly, there was a massive earthquake, and the prison was shaken to its foundations. All the doors immediately flew open, and the chains of every prisoner fell off!"*

Paul and Silas praised God even when their backs were bleeding and their feet and hands were in chains. Despite the pain and suffering they were going through, they praised God anyway; and as a result, God shook the very foundations of the prison, setting them free. God will shake the foundation of your prison; your bondage, your problem...if you make a decision to praise and give Him thanks, no matter what.

Praising God should become second–nature for all Believers. "This shall be written for the generation to come: and the people which shall be created shall praise the Lord" (Psalm 102:18). We were created to praise God, and it becomes a natural expression of your love for the Father when you spend time in the Word and meditate on His goodness.

When you have a heart for God and you know He loves you, your confidence in His ability to deliver you soars. You know help is on the way and you eagerly anticipate it.

First Thessalonians 5:16–18 encourages, *"Always be joyful. Never stop praying. Be thankful in all circumstances, for this is God's will for you who belong to Christ Jesus"* (NLT). God doesn't tell you to thank Him for negative circumstances; He says to thank Him while you're in the midst of them. Doing this shows that you trust Him to bring you out.

The storms of life are going to come; but don't let them disturb your peace and affect your thoughts and emotions. This will only move you into self–pity and frustration. Instead, maintain an attitude of praise.

Your first line of defense is the Word of God. Meditate on it and give it life by speaking it over your circumstances. If you need healing meditate on scriptures that reveal God's ability to heal. Receive that Word in your spirit and begin praising God for your healing.

The Word of God declares,

"Rejoice in the Lord always. I will say it again: Rejoice! Let your gentleness be evident to all. The Lord is near. Do not be anxious about anything, but in everything, by prayer and petition, with thanksgiving, present your requests to God. And the peace of God, which transcends all understanding, will guard your hearts and your minds in Christ Jesus"
(Philippians 4:4–7, NIV).

When you are in a situation and there seems to be no way out, open your mouth and praise the Lord—and don't stop. Instead of crying and complaining, give God praise because you know He has a plan for you that includes rising above the circumstances, restoration, and peace. Thank Him for His goodness because your praise will stop the enemy and give glory to the Lord God.

When your victory comes, continue to praise Him because He has more in store for you. Thank Him for blessing in your home, on your job and with your children. Declare your authority in Jesus, and watch God show up in your life in ways you would have never imagined.

HEBREWS 8:6

now He has obtained a more excellent ministry, inasmuch as He is also Mediator of a better covenant, which was established on better promises.

Chapter 13

LIVING THE ABUNDANT LIFE

T he Lord God has made provision for every Christian to live in
victory and abundance.

It's true that many Christians have not experienced victory in
their lives, but that doesn't mean that God has not provided it. He
has done everything in His power to give His children the authority
and provision needed to live triumphantly on the earth.

> *Whatever is born of God overcomes the world. And
> this is the victory that has overcome the world—our
> faith. Who is he who overcomes the world, but he
> who believes that Jesus is the Son of God?*
>
> 1 John 5:4-5

God doesn't give victory over the world to just a select few. He
has given victory to every person who is "born again." It's a gift
from God just as salvation is a gift from God. It cannot be earned
or merited, only received by faith. That's why the verse says the
victory is in our faith – our believing, receiving, confessing, and
doing the Word of God in Christ Jesus. (Matthew 7:24-25; Mark
11:22-25; 1 Timothy 6:12-13.)

Victory Is a Gift

> *Thanks be to God, who gives us the victory through
> our Lord Jesus Christ.*
>
> 1 Corinthians 15:57

No one can glory in their victories. All credit goes to God. He deserves our thankfulness. Through Christ and His Word we have victory over sin, sickness, depression, sorrow, fear, worry, and poverty.

When Jesus arose triumphantly from the grave, He won a complete victory over all the forces of darkness. He did it for us! It was mankind that needed victory in this life. So Jesus "made Himself of no reputation, taking the form of a bondservant, and coming in the likeness of men" (Philippians 2:7). He was your substitute. His victory was your victory.

> *Now thanks be to God who always leads us in triumph in Christ.*
>
> 2 Corinthians 2:14a

He Has Freely Given All Things

> *He who did not spare His own Son, but delivered Him up for us all, how shall He not with Him also freely give us all things?*
>
> Romans 8:32

If God gave you the most priceless possession He had, (Jesus), why would He withhold anything of less value? It is His desire to give you everything you need in this life and the life to come. Of course, you will be involved in working and laboring in various ways. But it will be God who gives the increase through different means to "freely give us all things."

Blessed With Every Spiritual Blessings

> *Blessed be the God and Father of our Lord Jesus Christ, who has blessed us with every spiritual blessing in the heavenly places in Christ.*
>
> Ephesians 1:3

God has already blessed us with every spiritual blessing for this life. Spiritual blessings will always manifest in physical abundance and provision. (When you activate them!)

God's blessings are available to you now. Possibly "you do not have because you do ask," or "you ask and do not receive, because you ask amiss, that you may spend it on your own pleasures" (James 4:2-3).

The primary reason in asking for God's blessings should be to share them with others. When your need is met abundantly, you have more than enough to share with those around you.

Every Need Supplied

God's will is for you to prosper in every way. A person can be a loyal and sincere Christian without prospering in every area of life. One could even be very successful in some areas without claiming "all" of God's promises. But why would any Christian not want all God has provided?

All the provisions of God are needed to be "fruitful in every good work . . ." (Colossians 1:10).

The first place you are to prosper is in your spirit life. As the *"law of the Spirit of life in Christ Jesus"* begins to rule in your heart — it will set you "free from the law of sin and death" that would try to enslave you mentally, physically, spiritually, and financially (Romans 8:2).

> *My God shall supply all your need according to His*
> *riches in glory by Christ Jesus.*
>
> Philippians 4:19

God is your source. He supplies your need. The basis for that supply is all of His riches in glory by Christ Jesus. The supply is unlimited. As you "seek first the Kingdom of God and His righteousness, all these things shall be added unto you" (Matthew 6:33).

Abundant Life in Christ Jesus

Jesus came to restore the relationship and fellowship between God and mankind. His desire is for man to enjoy the full abundant provisions of being part of God's family. But there is also a spiritual enemy who wants to keep you from living in your abundant provisions; Satan.

Jesus Himself presented this all-inclusive dichotomy.

> *The thief does not come except to steal, and to kill,*
> *and to destroy. I have come that they may have life,*
> *and that they may have it more abundantly.*
>
> John 10:10

The life that Jesus gives is abundant provision in every area of your life – spiritual, mental, physical, financial. You and I will progressively enjoy God's blessings when we steadfastly live by and give first place to Christ and His Word.

> *Beloved, I pray that you may prosper in all things*
> *and be in health, just as your soul prospers.*
>
> 3 John 2

Abounding In Every Good Work

As you give your life totally to the Lord and His Kingdom, you know that He will gladly give you all of His life. The Christian who gives his best to God and expects God's best, becomes extremely useful in the work of the Kingdom.

> *God is able to make all grace abound toward you,*
> *that you, always having all sufficiency in all things,*
> *may have an abundance for every good work.*
>
> 2 Corinthians 9:8

The most important thing to remember in living the abundant life is, "be a giver" – first to God, then to your fellow man. God will see to it that you abound in everything "that pertains to life and godliness" (2 Peter 1:3).

The Lord God will supply everything you need and make His grace abound in you, so that you will never lack in any good work to which He calls you.

God's Formula for Success (His way!)

Living in the kingdom of God has abundant benefits. As Believers, we must make it a priority to do things God's way so we can access what He has made available to us through His Word.

There is a formula for success in the kingdom of God, and if we follow it, we will get consistent results. This requires a renewing of our minds and a willingness to do things differently.

> *Do not be conformed to this world, but be transformed by the renewing of your mind, that you may prove what is that good and acceptable and perfect will of God.*
>
> Romans 12:2

God's method of operation is completely different from the world's way. It requires faith, diligence, and consistency in executing certain spiritual principles. By following 3 basic steps from God's Word, we can see manifestation in our lives, not some of the time, but all the time.

The first step in God's formula for success is to "meditate on God's Word." Meditation is simply pondering, considering, and muttering the Word of God.

When we meditate on God's Word, it expands our capacity for faith and transforms our ability to believe and receive. By meditating on the Word we focus our thoughts and set our hearts on the desired result we are seeking.

Psalm 1:1-3 says that the man who is empowered to prosper is the one who meditates on the Word day and night. This is the same approach we should take while spending time seriously pondering the Scriptures.

We can meditate the Word by applying it practically to our lives, putting ourselves in agreement with it, speaking it, and realizing its integrity. Meditating on the Word makes our way prosperous (Joshua 1:8).

The second step to success in the kingdom of God is to "speak God's Word." Many times, a person's heart is full of faith but that faith never gets released into the atmosphere because he or she doesn't actually say what God has said! Speaking the Word of God is critical to getting results in the kingdom.

Death and life are in the power of the tongue, and if you're not saying anything, you're not creating anything. (Proverbs 18:21.) Keeping the Word in our mouths at all times is vital because of the creative power of words. (Mark 11:23; Luke 6:45.)

Hebrews 10:23 says, *"Let us hold fast the profession of our faith without wavering."*

Our "profession" is our confession, or what we "say and pray" from the Word of God. We should make this a daily practice.

Continually speaking God's Word through regular confessions also repels the enemy. Satan cannot stand against a Believer who has a revelation of the power of speaking the Word.

Jesus gave us the example of speaking the Word:

> *Now when the tempter came to Him, he said, "If You are the Son of God, command that these stones become bread."* [4] *But He answered and said, "It is written, 'Man shall not live by bread alone, but by every word that proceeds from the mouth of God.*
>
> Matthew 4:3-4

The third step in God's formula for success is to "act on the Word of God." Faith without works is dead, which means it is not enough to simply hear the Word and believe it, but we must also act on it in order to get to our destination. Faith is a practical expression of our confidence in God and His Word. Many times, Christians get preoccupied with the spiritual side of things and neglect to do anything practical in the natural realm. When God speaks a Word, whether through the written scriptures or a *rhema* Word spoken to the heart, it requires some type of corresponding action on our part.

God's formula for success is fail-proof. Speaking the Word releases faith, meditating on it builds the image of it on the inside of you, and stepping out on what the Word says connects you to the promised manifestation. The result is success and absolute victory in every area of your life!

Attend to God's Word

Sometimes we can become so fixed on receiving new revelation from God that we allow some of the basic principles we've learned to slip. Faith, the importance of speaking God's Word, and the power of the blood of Jesus are some of the fundamental principles of Christianity that we should constantly put ourselves in remembrance of.

Another important principle that Believers must keep at the forefront of their thinking is the importance of attending to God's Word. In the daily hustle and bustle of life, it can become easy to allow our time spent studying and meditating on the Word to decrease. We must make a consistent effort to keep first things first in our lives, which means daily attending to God's Word.

As Believers, we know Jesus came so we could live the abundant life (John 10:10). We also know that the just shall live by faith. So, what is the connecting factor to living this abundant life the Bible promises?

The answer is found in Proverbs 4:20-22, which says, *"give attention to my words; Incline your ear to my sayings. Do not let them depart from your eyes; Keep them in the midst of your heart; For they are life to those who find them, And health to all their flesh."*

When we pay close attention to the Word, and internalize it, abundant life will flow out of us.

We must make a quality decision to commit to the Word and consistently obey it. That's the way we access the abundant life, which translates as total life prosperity, or success in every area of life. We must be doers of the Word to get any results.

So, how do we attend to the Word of God? Well, the definition of attend is "to direct and apply oneself; to pay attention," according to Webster's Dictionary. Every day, we must allow our time spent with the Word to be our priority.

On a practical level, it means spending time reading the Bible before we step out of the house in the morning, being consistent in making confessions of faith at some point during the day. We listen to the Word being preached regularly, and allowing God's way of doing things to be the basis for how we handle the situations we face throughout the day.

When we attend to the Word, there is the potential for us to produce great results in our lives.

In Mark 4:20, Jesus says, *"And these are they which are sown on good ground; such as hear the Word, and receive it, and bring forth fruit, some thirtyfold, some sixty, and some an hundred."*

In verse 23-24, He says, *"If anyone has ears to hear, let him hear."* Then He said to them, *"Take heed what you hear. With the same measure you use, it will be measured to you; and to you who hear, more will be given."*

Any person who has ears to hear (inclined, fixed to hear, and act on what God says) will receive even more from the Lord! That is the abundant, overflowing life that Jesus came to give us.

Attending to God's Word means taking God at His Word, fully trusting that what He said, He will do. It means casting all our cares on Him and choosing to think on the promises of God at all times.

When we attend to the Word, we don't allow the news reports or the media to affect our faith. We don't make plans based on what the world system tells us, but we frame our life through the Word of God.

If we would begin to refocus our attention on God's Word, and commit to making it the centerpiece of our lives, we will begin to see some amazing things begin to happen in our circumstances. The Word contains the life force of God that has the ability to eradicate anything that does not line up with the blessing. Attend to the Word and you will see results!

Activate Your Abundant Life in Christ Today!

1. Born again. (John 3:3-6; Romans 10:9; 1 Peter 1:23.)
2. Spirit filled. (Luke 11:13; John 14:15-17, 26; John 16:13-14; Acts 1:8; Acts 2:1-4; Acts 19:2.)
3. Abide in the Word. (John 8:31-32; Joshua 1:8; Psalm 1:1-3; John 15:7; Colossians 3:15-16; 1 Timothy 3:16; 3 John 2.)
4. Doer of the Word. (John 14:21, 23; James 1:22.)
5. Live by Faith. (Romans 1:17; 1 Cor. 5:7; Hebrews 10:38.)
6. Walk in Love. (1 Corinthians 13; Galatians 5:22; 1 John 4:7-8.)
7. Walk in the Spirit. (Galatians 5:16, 25.)
8. Cheerful giver. (*Malachi 3:6-12, Galatians 6:6-7; Luke 6:38; Proverbs 3:9; 2 Corinthians 9:5-8; Hebrews 7:1-28.*)
9. Pray and Speak the Word. (Matthew 4:3-11; Matthew 8:5-10; Mark 11:22-25; Romans 4:17; Luke 6:45; 1 Timothy 6:12-13.)

Chapter 14

STRONGER, GROWING FAITH

Living the Faith Life

L iving by faith is not an option for the Believer; it is a way of life. God's Word is the governing force of His Kingdom, and this Kingdom operates by specific laws and principles. One of those spiritual principles includes the law of faith. Faith is the currency that enables you to receive the promises of God and the blessings of His Kingdom. As a child of the King, you must use faith to access what is available to you in the spiritual realm.

There are two systems in operation in the Earth: the Kingdom of God system and the world's system. The Kingdom of God is governed by Jesus Christ; He is Lord of this system. It is founded on love and operates by faith. It is higher than the world's system. On the other hand, the world's system is governed by Satan, and is founded on selfishness. Fear rules this system and is the spiritual force controlling those who live in it.

As children of God, we have to understand the way God has intended for us to operate on this Earth. We are in the world, but not *of* the world. We are ambassadors of Heaven, occupying the Earth until Jesus returns. We are His representatives and He expects us to demonstrate His power and ability to the world, so those in that system are drawn to Him. Faith is the only way to accomplish this.

Many Christians today do not live by faith. The reason is that faith is the substance of things hoped for, and the evidence of things not seen. Therefore, it should be no surprise when what you believe from the Bible is not immediately available to your physical senses. In fact, you should know when you set out on your faith walk, that you do not need to see things with your physical eyes because your faith is the proof that what you believe exists!

Everything in the natural realm originates in the spiritual realm. When you have faith, you are able to see everything Heaven has to offer you without "seeing" it in front of you first. By tapping into faith, you gain access to the abundant life, prosperity, health, and blessings available to you. Anything you find in the Word of God is available to you in Heaven's storehouses; from wisdom to finances.

Abiding in the Kingdom of God means living by faith on a consistent basis. The systems of this world are failing and falling apart. Those in the Kingdom of God have an advantage because of their faith in God's Word. Find out what God says about you and believe it! That is what living the faith life is all about.

What Is Faith?

In order to directly lay hold of God's promises, you must use faith. You release your faith by acting out on what you believe from God's Word. Faith is a practical expression of your confidence in God and the Word's ability to produce a harvest. When you act on your beliefs, you will begin to see the results you desire.

Faith is an act that is motivated by the Word of God, whether written or spoken. Whenever God tells you to do something and you obey, you demonstrate your faith. It is corresponding action that lines up with what you believe. For example, if you are sick and believing God for healing, take the medicine your doctor has prescribed and confess the Word of God on healing.

You can tell what people believe by how they act. Have you ever met someone who had extremely high confidence? This person carries himself or herself in a way that conveys a sense of authority. There is a certain air about a person who is confident; it is undeniable.

The same is true where your faith is concerned. A person who has faith constantly speaks the Word of God and acts as if what he or she is believing for has already come to pass. (Romans 4:17.)

The key however, is to not to do something foolish and call it faith; this is presumption. Make sure you find the promise in God's Word and that if you have heard Him speak directly to your heart about something, that what you hear and receive lines up with the scripture.

James 2:17, 18 describes the importance of acting out on your faith: *"faith by itself, if it does not have works, is dead. But someone will say, "You have faith, and I have works." Show me your faith without your works, and I will show you my faith by my works."*

You see, faith has to have action behind it.

For example, if you are believing God for financial increase, don't just confess prosperity scriptures and expect for your checking account balance to miraculously increase overnight. Do something to demonstrate your expectation of God's promise; open a savings account and begin to exercise good stewardship over the money you already have. In addition, don't neglect to pay your tithes and give offerings according to what God speaks to your heart. Taking actions such as these give practical expression to what you believe from the Word.

Faith Or Foolishness

Too many Christians get spiritually "foolish" and do silly things that they label as "walking by faith." For example, someone may write a bad check, claiming they have faith in God to provide the money before the check clears. These actions aren't faith; they are foolishness. God will never tell you to do something that is illegal.

The Bible is full of accounts of people who heard God speak to them and had to act out on their faith. Noah was one of them. Hebrews 11:7 describes his faith, *"By faith Noah, being warned of God of things not seen as yet, moved with fear, prepared an ark to the saving of his house..."* In John 2:1–11, the servants at the wedding at Cana released their faith by obeying Jesus' instructions, and a creative miracle took place—water was turned into wine. In both instances, these people demonstrated their belief by doing something specific; their faith could be seen.

To keep your faith strong, continue to seek God and feed your spirit the Word of God on a consistent basis. In addition, don't speak negative words or act contrary to what you believe. Keep your words *and* actions in line with what you believe and you will be actively demonstrating your faith in God and His Word. God weighs your actions, so make sure He sees your faith today!

Keep the Faith

Evidence is defined as "something that indicates" or gives "an outward sign." In a court of law, the evidence you present to a judge can mean the difference between prison and freedom, or in some cases, life and death. In the kingdom of God, the evidence you present to your heavenly Father will determine whether or not you receive from Him the things you desire. When it comes to proving to God that you are ready to receive all that He has predestined for you, *faith* is the most compelling evidence you can present to Him.

The term faith is sometimes used as if it means "belief" or "hope." But faith is really much more than either of these words suggest. According to Hebrews 11:1, "...*faith is the substance of things hoped for, the evidence of things not seen.*" In other words, faith is *knowing* that the things you hope for "belong" to you, even when you don't see any outward signs that they exist. Believers often sincerely "hope" that God will help them—they even pray for hours—but nothing happens without faith. If you don't understand faith, you won't know how to operate in God's system.

Faith Pleases God

Imagine that you need money to pay your car note. You've tried several options, but they've all failed. Now you're desperate and you need God to "work a miracle" on your behalf. What are your options? You could cry, feel sorry for yourself and say, "I'm a good person. Why doesn't God just help me?" If you take this approach, God will see you crying and sympathize with you, but His Word says, "*Without faith it is impossible to please him...*" (Hebrews 11:6), so your emotional expression is unlikely to change anything.

To get God to act on your behalf, you could choose to pray a traditional "religious" prayer: *"Lord, You work in mysterious ways. Please stop by my house, God. Please! Please, Father. Please don't pass me by...."* This is the way many people pray, but this type of prayer doesn't express faith. It has the form of a prayer, but it lacks the power to produce results. James 1:6 (*AMP*) says that we must ask in faith without wavering or doubting.

As a Believer, you have the right to receive answers to every one of your prayers. But the key to getting answers is faith. Whenever you pray or call upon God to help you, you must present evidence of your faith.

For example, if you want God to show you how to get your car note paid, you have to petition Him correctly: *"Father, your Word says that You will supply all of my needs according to Your riches in heaven. I ask you, Father, to show me how to pay my car note. I surrender this problem to you, and I know that it is already resolved. I thank You, Father, for answering my prayer."* A faith–filled prayer that is firmly rooted in God's Word will get answers!

Faith comes by hearing the Word of God, so build your faith by spending time reading and studying the Word. God's Word (His book of promises) is the evidence you must present to receive the answers you need. His Word is your confession. It is the thing you say to Him in prayer, thereby increasing your faith. Pick up your Bible and find scriptures to match the things you're petitioning God for. Using His Word assures your response.

When you know what the Word says about the things you are promised to receive, you can pray for those things and receive the answers you need. You never have to beg, plead or bargain with God to have Him answer your prayers. He is moved by your faith in His Word. Show God your faith, and He will show you His love by pouring out His blessings in your life and fulfilling all of the promises He made in His Word.

Fearless Faith

Have you ever noticed that we live in a fear—based society? All you have to do is turn on the news or read the newspaper, and you'll see that doubt and fear have peaked and become the pattern for millions. People are afraid they'll die of cancer, afraid they won't be able to pay their bills, afraid they're going to lose their jobs, afraid they'll never have children. What's worse, many people have been deceived into believing that fear is just as normal as breathing, but I beg to differ. Fear is anything but normal!

Fear is actually tainted or contaminated faith. While faith is a practical demonstration of confidence in God and His Word, fear is a practical demonstration of confidence in Satan and his word. Every day we must ask ourselves, *who am I connected to—God or Satan?* If we want to be connected with God, we've got to have faith. Conversely, we must consciously realize that if we are void of faith and full of fear, we're actually connected to Satan. Just as God uses faith to gain access into our lives, Satan perverts faith and uses fear to gain entry into our lives.

Every day fear and faith are in an unyielding battle to reign supreme in our lives. When people accept or tolerate fear, they're unwittingly being lured into Satan's plan to control their lives. However, using the Word of God to abolish fear creates and develops fearless faith that is bold and unstoppable, and it's that faith which allows you to obtain the victory God has given you through His Son, Jesus Christ.

Did you know your born—again spirit is not even capable of producing fear? God has not given you the spirit of fear which leads to bondage. In fact, He's freed you from bondage, and He doesn't want you going back to it. So, if fear doesn't come from inside you, where does it come from? Fear is produced and comes as a result of things you've learned, heard, seen, and experienced. It is a byproduct of your soul—your mind, will, and emotions—which is the area Satan desperately wants to control.

Ultimately Satan uses fear to cause you to think God's Word won't come to pass. If you fear God's Word won't come to pass, then you most certainly are not operating in faith. And if you are not operating in faith, you're not connected to God.

Now do you see why it's imperative to uproot fear and the spirit of doubt from your life? I urge you to do whatever needs to be done to abolish fear from every area of your life, now! Pray and ask God to lead you to the source of your fears. Attacking your fears from the source literally destroys them at the root, and creates a foundation for fearless faith.

Relentless Faith

What does it mean to have "bulldog faith"? It's the type of belief that grabs on to the promises of God and refuses to let go. It is relentless. Every Christian is called to live their lives by releasing the faith of God into their situations and circumstances. Everyone will face temptations, trials, and tests, but only those who refuse to let go of what God has said will see the end of their faith. A relentless Christian is the one who gets results in the Kingdom of God.

When you look at that word, *relentless*, it really denotes a sense of steadfastness, perseverance, and a refusal to give up, cave in, or quit. It simply will *not* come off the promises of God. It is focused in its pursuit of the final outcome—no matter what it goes through or faces. A person who is relentless is a real soldier where the things of God are concerned and in the way they handle the devil. This person is not easily swayed by what things look like or how they feel. They have locked into the faith of God, and you had better believe manifestation is on its way!

The key to walking in relentless faith is to refuse to entertain unbelief. Faith will not work when you have doubt in your heart. You must stand firm on the promises from God's Word and reject any thought, suggestion, or inclination that goes against what you believe. The enemy will bring negative thoughts to your mind, but you can override them by knowing and quoting the Scripture.

Believe and Receive

Jesus gave an important formula for getting your faith to work—every time! He said it is critical to believe you receive what you pray for, when you say it, and do not allow doubt to invade your heart and mind.

When you do this, you can move mountains! To be relentless in your faith means fighting doubt and unbelief the moment they come to your mind, filling your heart with the Word of God, and speaking it at every turn with boldness, authority, and consistency. Doing this creates a pounding spiritual force that blows obstacles out of your way.

Knowing Who You Are In Christ

To operate in this kind of faith, you must know who you are in Christ. Christians have been made righteous by the blood of Jesus and are no longer under the dominion of sin and the curse. Consequently, you have a right to every covenant promise in God's Word, including the benefits of faith-based living. In fact, living by faith is a requirement, not an option for those who are a part of God's Kingdom.

Walking by faith is an adventure that will take you on a treasure hunt through the Word of God. Your faith is your ammunition against Satan and will carry you through tough times. Refuse to give up, even in the face of adversity. When you have relentless, bulldog faith, nothing will be withheld from you!

Confess the Word

Have you ever been faced with a situation that looked and seemed impossible? All of us will go through challenges and circumstances that test our faith to the utmost extent. The key to overcoming impossible situations is to stay in faith and refuse to move from your stand on the Word of God. Whatever you may be going through, there is a promise in the Bible that provides the answer. You simply must not waver when the enemy tries to distract your focus.

One of the keys to maintaining strong faith in the midst of afflictions and tough circumstances is to continually confess God's Word. Confession of the Word not only releases the power of God into the situation, but it builds faith into your heart, which enables you to weather the storms of life.

Man is a tri-part being—he is a spirit who possesses a soul, and lives in a physical body. The spirit of man is where faith resides and from which faith proceeds. When you confess God's Word, you hear yourself saying the Scriptures and the faith of God is deposited in your spirit. The Word, when planted in your heart like seed in soil, will produce results.

You Have Victory In Christ

Everything necessary for victory in life has been deposited in the born again spirit of a man. That means that when we face impossible situations we shouldn't be waiting on God to do something; we should tap into the power that is already within us. Ephesians 1:3 says, *"Blessed be the God and Father of our Lord Jesus Christ, who has blessed us with every spiritual blessing in the heavenly places in Christ."*

Healing, deliverance, abundance, and prosperity in spirit, soul, and body are spiritual blessings that belong to us. When we make Jesus the Lord of our lives, we obtain an inheritance of spiritual resources that are designed to equip us to dominate in the earth.

Getting a revelation of what already belongs to us is critical to being an overcomer in life. We even possess the spirit of might, which is the ability to do anything. The Word says that we have received the fullness of His power (John 1:16). Knowing this, we can no longer go through life defeated by what the enemy throws at us. Whether it is sickness and disease, poverty, lack, or emotional oppression, we have the victory.

Unleashing the power and faith of God requires consistently confessing God's Word. This should be a regular part of every Christian's life. Philemon 1:4-6 says that we should acknowledge every good thing that is within us.

Essentially, this means we are to declare what we possess spiritually through our relationship with Jesus, the Christ. If we need healing, we should declare that the healing power of God is resident in our reborn spirits. If it is prosperity we need, we should confess that prosperity belongs to us according to the Word of God. To confess something means to acknowledge, or admit that it is true. When we confess the Word we are making a declaration that it is the final authority in our lives.

Confessing the Word is a key way to stay in faith, especially when the appearance of the situation looks bleak. Believers are to walk by faith, not by what they perceive with their five senses. The spiritual realm, what we possess in our spirits, and the Word of God are more real than anything we might see in the natural realm.

If we refuse to come off the Word, we will see the end of our faith.

The primary attack every person faces when they are in a faith battle is the enemy attempting to use the things we perceive with our senses to move us from our stance on the Word.

It's the time period between releasing our faith and seeing the actual manifestation that is where the biggest fight occurs. No matter what Satan does to try and distract you, don't come off the Word.

If you stay in faith and keep your mind focused on the Lord, He will bring you out with flying colors. Victory belongs to the person who refuses to let go of the Word.

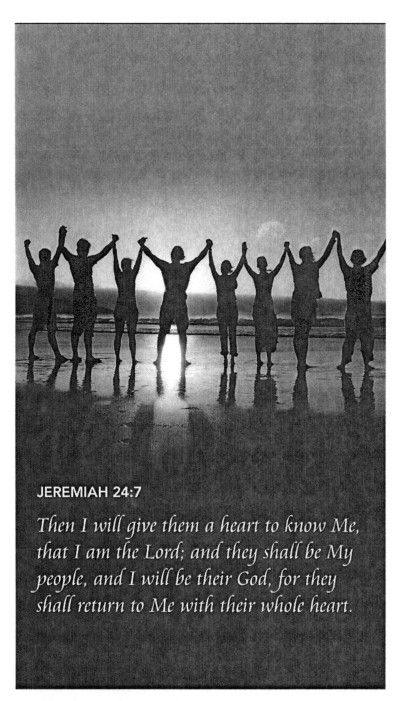

JEREMIAH 24:7

Then I will give them a heart to know Me, that I am the Lord; and they shall be My people, and I will be their God, for they shall return to Me with their whole heart.

Chapter 15

"Expectation" is the Key

"Expectation" is the breeding ground for living in the supernatural. In order to receive from the Lord, we must *expect* Him to show up and show out in our lives. Without a fervent sense of expectancy, all we are doing is taking part in religious exercises that have no power behind them. It's time for Believers to start expecting God to do some great and mighty things in our lives.

Many Christians pray, read their Bibles, go to church, and serve in various capacities in ministry, but when it comes to the promises of God leaping off the pages of the Bible and manifesting in their lives, their faith levels are really low. They say they believe but they really do not, nor do they really expect God to come through on His Word. This is not the way Christians should live.

God wants us to release our faith for *everything* we need and desire. He wants you to expand your capacity to receive by believing Him for BIG things! When you read a scripture from His Word, and receive it in your heart, without doubt, you should absolutely *expect* it to come to pass. There should be no question in your mind that what God said is exactly what He will do.

I like the example of the man at the Gate called Beautiful, in the book of Acts.

Acts 3:2-5 recounts the scene:

> *"A certain man lame from his mother's womb was carried, whom they laid daily at the gate of the temple which is called Beautiful, to ask alms from those who entered the temple; who, seeing Peter and John about to go into the temple, asked for alms. ⁴ And*

*fixing his eyes on him, with John, Peter said, "Look
at us." So he gave them his attention, expecting to
receive something from them."*

This man received his healing because he "expected" to get
something from Peter and John. (Of course he was expecting money,
but he received something far better!). As a result, he was able to
leap to his feet.

A Woman Breaks the Time Barrier

I wonder how many Christians could have already experienced
the manifestation of the things they are believing from the Word, if
only they would walk in "unwavering expectation." There are no
limits to what God can do, and if you can believe for what seems
impossible, He will do it.

> *"Now a certain woman had a flow of blood for twelve
> years, and had suffered many things from many
> physicians. She had spent all that she had and was
> no better, but rather grew worse. When she heard
> about Jesus, she came behind Him in the crowd and
> touched His garment. For she said, "If only I may
> touch His clothes, I shall be made well."*
>
> Mark 5:25-28

Now this woman could have given up after waiting for 12 long
years. But after hearing of Jesus, her expectations were raised to a
new level. She began to declare a positive-faith confession! Here's
the result:

> *"Immediately the fountain of her blood was dried up,
> and she felt in her body that she was healed of the
> affliction."*
>
> Mark 5:29.

Then Jesus said to her:

"Daughter, your faith has made you well. Go in peace, and be healed of your affliction."

Don't limit God because of what your past experiences have been, or based on what others may say. Sometimes you will have to get "out of the box" so to speak, in order to receive bigger and better things from God. If you can find it in the Word of God, and you have the faith for it, you will possess it. You are not waiting on God; He is waiting on you! Walk in expectation and watch your dreams become a reality.

Expectant Faith

Expectant faith is "bulldog faith"! It is the type of belief that grabs on to the promises of God and refuses to let go. It is relentless. Every Christian is called to live their lives by releasing the faith of God into their situations and circumstances. Everyone will face temptations, trials, and tests, but only those who refuse to let go of what God has promised will see the end of their faith. An expectant Christian is the one who gets results in the Kingdom of God.

When you look at that word, *expectation*, it denotes a sense of anticipation of something good; with a flavor of steadfastness, perseverance, and a refusal to give up, cave in, or quit. It simply will *not* come off the promises of God. It is focused in its pursuit of the final outcome—no matter what it goes through or faces. A person who lives with expectation is a real soldier where the things of God are concerned and in the way they handle the devil. This person is not easily swayed by what things look like or how they feel. They have locked into the faith of God, and you had better believe manifestation is on its way!

"We do not look at the things which are seen, but at the things which are not seen. For the things which are seen are temporary, but the things which are not seen are eternal."

2 Corinthians 4:18

The key to living with expectant faith is to refuse to entertain unbelief. Faith will not work when you have doubt in your heart. You must stand firm on the promises from God's Word and reject any thought, suggestion, or inclination that goes against what you believe. The enemy will bring negative thoughts to your mind, but you can override them by knowing and quoting the Scripture.

Jesus gave an important formula for getting your faith to work—every time! He said it is critical to believe you receive what you pray for, when you say it, and do not allow doubt to invade your heart and mind. When you do this, you can move mountains!

> *"Whoever says to this mountain, 'Be removed and be cast into the sea,' and does not doubt in his heart, but believes that those things he says will be done, he will have whatever he says. Therefore I say to you, whatever things you ask when you pray, believe that you receive them, and you will have them."*
>
> Mark 11:23-24

To be expectant in your faith means fighting doubt and unbelief the moment they come to your mind, filling your heart with the Word of God, and speaking it at every turn with boldness, authority, and consistency. Doing this creates a pounding spiritual force that "breaks barriers" out of your way.

To operate in this kind of faith, you must know who you are in Christ. Christians have been made righteous by the blood of Jesus and are no longer under the dominion of sin and the curse. Consequently, you have a right to every covenant promise in God's Word, including the benefits of faith-based living. In fact, living by faith is a requirement, not an option for those who are a part of God's Kingdom.

Living your faith with expectancy is an adventure that will take you on a treasure hunt through the Word of God. Your faith is your ammunition against Satan and will carry you through tough times. Refuse to give up, even in the face of adversity. When you have positive faith expectation, nothing will be withheld from you!

Confess What You Expect

God has given us a powerful method to obtain His promises, and it is up to us to use it. That method is confession. Confession, as it pertains to the Bible, is when you speak the Word of God out loud. Words are spiritual containers that release either fear or faith. Every time you speak, you are activating spiritual forces that will affect your life. This is why it is so important to be mindful of the words we speak and to make sure we are only saying what God has said in His Word.

Similar to the law of gravity, the law of confession will work for anyone who will get involved with it. Many Christians who have been defeated in life are defeated because they believe and confess the wrong things. They don't realize that their words are activating a spiritual law that is working against them. We must understand the law of confession if we want things to work for us. We have been given access to the power of God through our words, which are weapons against the enemy.

Satan is constantly applying pressure to our minds in order to get us to quit in these last days; however, we do not have to allow hard times or pressure to defeat us. We can use the Word of God as a weapon against the enemy, and win.

In order to be victorious over the attacks of the enemy, we must think, believe, and speak in line with God's Word. In fact, believing the Word in our hearts is the prerequisite for our confessions having a significant impact in our lives.

> *Jesus said to him, "If you can believe, all things are possible to him who believes."*
>
> Mark 9:23

Faith is the force that must be in operation in order for our confessions to come to pass.

Sometimes people confess God's Word religiously, mechanically, and out of fear; however, these types of confessions don't accomplish anything. We must believe that the things we confess from the Bible are coming to pass as we pray and speak them.

We can look to God as an example of how faith-filled words cause things to manifest in the natural realm. In the biblical account of how God created the earth, the Word says that He spoke and whatever He spoke came into existence (Genesis 1). God's words are full of faith, which is what caused them to become actual physical substance. The things we see in this earth today, from the sky to the trees, are the result of words that were spoken by God.

The same creative power that God possesses has been invested in us. As spiritual beings who possess the nature of God, we have the ability to speak things into existence just like God did.

This isn't some mystical, New Age idea; it is scriptural. When Jesus walked the earth, He imitated His Father by speaking what the Father spoke. As a result, He saw results everywhere He went. Likewise, we must be imitators of God, who think, act, and speak like Him. When we speak His Words, we release His creative ability into the earth, and something always happens. When we believe beyond a shadow of a doubt that the words we speak will come to pass, we will see what we are speaking.

> *"Since we have the same spirit of faith, according to what is written, "I believed and therefore I spoke," we also believe and therefore speak."*
>
> 2 Corinthians 4:13

> *". . . he believed—God, who gives life to the dead and calls those things which do not exist as though they did."*
>
> Romans 4:17b

The Bible says that all things are possible for those who believe. Confessing God's Word is empowering because every time we hear ourselves speaking the Scriptures, we are actually planting faith in our hearts. The more we become established on the Word of God through speaking it on a consistent basis, the more our faith will grow. And faith, when acted upon, will always produce the desired results.

There shouldn't be a day that passes that the Believer does not speak the Word of God. It is the Word that strengthens our faith, and releases the power of God into our situations and circumstances. By making daily confessions, we frame our worlds with the Word of God, shut the devil out of our lives, and plant faith in our hearts. It is the key to raising our expectations and "breaking barriers!"

"No Fear" – "Yes Expectation"

Have you ever noticed that we live in a fear-based society? All you have to do is turn on the news or read the newspaper, and you'll see that doubt and fear have peaked and become the pattern for millions. People are afraid they'll die of cancer, afraid they won't be able to pay their bills, afraid they're going to lose their jobs, afraid they'll never have children. What's worse, many people have been deceived into believing that fear is just as normal as breathing, but I beg to differ. Fear is anything but normal!

Fear is actually tainted or contaminated faith. While faith is a practical demonstration of confidence in God and His Word, fear is a practical demonstration of confidence in Satan and his word. Every day we must ask ourselves, *who am I connected to—God or Satan?* If we want to be connected with God, we've got to have faith.

Conversely, we must consciously realize that if we are void of faith and full of fear, we're actually connected to Satan. Just as God uses faith to gain access into our lives, Satan perverts faith and uses fear to gain entry into our lives.

Every day fear and faith are in an unyielding battle to reign supreme in our lives. When people accept or tolerate fear, they're unwittingly being lured into Satan's plan to control their lives. However, using the Word of God to abolish fear creates and develops "fearless expectation" that is bold and unstoppable, and it's that faith which allows you to obtain the victory God has given you through His Son, Jesus Christ.

Did you know your born-again spirit is not even capable of producing fear? God has not given you the spirit of fear which leads to bondage. In fact, He's freed you from bondage, and He doesn't want you going back to it. So, if fear doesn't come from inside you, where does it come from? Fear is produced and comes as a result of things you've learned, heard, seen, and experienced. It is a byproduct of your soul—your mind, will, and emotions—which is the area Satan desperately wants to control.

Ultimately Satan uses fear to cause you to think God's Word won't come to pass. If you fear God's Word won't come to pass, then you most certainly are not operating in faith. And if you are not operating in faith, you're not expecting—and if you're not expecting—barriers will remain.

Now do you see why it's imperative to uproot fear and the spirit of doubt from your life? I urge you to do whatever needs to be done to abolish fear from every area of your life, now! Pray and ask God to lead you to the source of your fears. Attacking your fears from the source literally destroys them at the root.

With positive expectation in Christ and His Word, you can create a foundation for "breaking every barrier" of sin, sickness, oppression, depression, lack, past hurts, or defeat in your life. You are an overcomer and more than a conqueror in Christ Jesus!

> *"Therefore submit to God. Resist the devil and he will flee from you."*
>
> James 4:7

Chapter 16

THE MOST POWERFUL FORCE IN THE UNIVERSE

There is nothing that we have, or will have, that is more powerful than our words. *"Death and life are in the power of the tongue,"* (Proverbs 18:21). God created us that way!

Almighty God could have chosen to swing His arm to create the universe.

He could have just had a thought and there would have been a world. But He chose His words and He said, *"Let there be light,"* and there was light.

Consider our prayers to God. He already knows our needs and desires. But there is something vitally important about expressing our thoughts by the spoken word.

Words of prayer (if it's according to the Word) carry the will of God to the earth. That's why the book of James teaches that we do not have because we do not ask, (James 4:2).

Many people go along day after day hoping nothing bad will happen that they cannot handle. Then, when something does happen, they try to change things with a few moments of prayers and tears.

The reality is that they might have been *forecasting* (or confessing) what happened by putting spiritual laws into motion.

How do we put spiritual laws into motion? Through the words we speak day after day.

Jesus taught that we can speak to mountains; (problems). We can tell them to *"be removed and be cast into the sea,"* and if we speak and do not doubt in our hearts, but believe that what we say will be done, we will have whatever we say; "confess." (See Mark 11:22-25.)

We should talk "to" the problem—not "about" the problem.

The overall Bible truth is — we will never rise above our confession of faith.

There Is a Miracle in Your Mouth

Your future is to experience the goodness of God. He created you with faith to overcome whatever comes your way in this life. God has given faith to every person—it is your job to believe. Throughout the ministry of Christ, He consistently promised that all things would be possible to anyone who believes. (See Mark 9:23.)

Our words can be a powerful tool used in our favor or they can also be an unruly and deadly force, causing our lives to be shipwrecked if we let them run out of control.

James 3:6 presents a powerful Bible truth on this matter:

> *"The tongue is a fire, a world of iniquity. The tongue is so set among our members that it defiles the whole body, and sets on fire the course of nature; and it is set on fire by hell."*

Our only hope for taming our tongues, and thereby charting a good course for our future, is the Word of God.

The Good Treasure

If we are going to use the Word of God to navigate through this life, there are a couple of issues we need to settle first.

How about those times when things are just not going your way? It may be in the area of marriage, finances, health, or work. Whatever it is, pressure seems to keep building until you feel like you're going to explode if you don't say something about it.

Why do you think it's so hard to keep our mouths under control in situations like that?

Jesus addressed this in the forth chapter of Mark. He warned that Satan comes to steal the Word of God from our hearts through persecution, offense, the cares of this world, the deceitfulness of riches, and lust. He uses everything in this natural realm to stir up our flesh and get us to open our mouths. (See Mark 4:14-20.)

So the issue comes down to this: What kind of words will we believe and speak?

The Bible explains it like this, *"For out of the abundance of the heart the mouth speaks. A good man out of the good treasure of his heart brings forth good things, and an evil man out of the evil treasure brings forth evil things,"* (Matthew 12:34-5).

It's not surprising that when we're under pressure from our flesh — being moved by what we see, feel, or think — we tend to open our mouths and say things like:

"I'm so unworthy," "I'm so tired," "I'm so sick," and "nothing good ever happens for me."

When the pressure is on, that's when we find out what's really inside us. And it should be the Word of God. Right?

Yet what we see, what we think, and what we say does not change the truth of God's Word. That's why James implied that trusting in facts and feelings is lying against the truth, or lying against the Word. (See James 3:14)

If we say anything other than what the Word of God says about a situation, we are lying against the truth.

Heaven Backs Your Words

You and I have a priest we can go to — and He's not just any priest. We have Jesus, our heavenly High Priest. *"Consider the Apostle and High Priest of our confession, Christ Jesus,"* (Hebrews 3:1).

God sent Jesus to be High Priest over our words of faith. That's why something we said last week — can come to pass this week.

Jesus is not going to speak words for us and have them come to pass in our lives. No, He has already spoken. So what can you and I do?

First, stop saying the same things the world says, like, *"Nothing good ever happens to me,"* or, *"I'm sick and tired of this or that."*

We expect people of this world to say things like that. That's exactly what they can expect in a life without Jesus. (But not us!)

If we believe that our words determine our future health, blessing, and place in eternity — we need to stop rehearsing what we don't want and start talking what we do want.

Second, we need to start filling our mouths with the Word of God. Make a *forecast* confession such as, *"I will* say *of the Lord, 'He is my refuge and my fortress; My God, in Him will I trust',"* (Psalm 91:2-3).

The challenge for us is to change from worldly, negative words to positive words of God's truth.

Start creating a better world for yourself today. Begin by speaking strong words that are for God, not against Him. Speak words that your High Priest can honor and then bring to pass.

You'll See It When You Believe It

The vast majority of people, including believers, don't know how to control the words that come out of their mouths.

Letting our words fly is the worst thing we can do when our lives seem out of control. Curses fly when we are in pain. Lies fly when we're trying to cover sin. Gossip flies when we try to make others think we are in control of our lives.

Murmuring and complaining are sometimes our substitutes for a good forecast of faith.

Letting words fly is a *forecast* of failure. Your words work in the negative as sure as they work in the positive.

Courageous words of faith in the face of any circumstance will activate the blessings of God.

Facts Change—Truth Doesn't

God's Word is "truth" and without hypocrisy (not a false assumption). God's Word overrides temporary facts!

That's why it is not wrong for you to have flu symptoms yet go around quoting God's Word, saying, *"By His stripes I was healed. Healing is mine, and I receive it now!"* (See 1Peter 2:24 and Isaiah 53:4-5.)

Sure, people may look at you and say, "That's a lie. You're sick."

But we're not going around declaring our physical health according to the Word in order to convince people there is nothing wrong with us. We're confessing God's Word to change what's wrong with our bodies. We're speaking God's Word after Him— and He *"calls those things which do not exist as though they did,"* (Romans 4:17).

Granted, we may *look* sick, and our bodies may show symptoms of sickness. But that is not the truth of the matter. That's not what God's Word says about the situation.

What's more, the truth—God's Word—is eternal. It never changes. Facts, on the other hand, do change. And it's the truth that changes them!

Keep the Right Focus

Don't misunderstand. Doctors can be your best friends. They are fighting the same enemy with medicine that God's Word is fighting. In fact, the apostle Luke wrote both the gospel of Luke and the book of Acts. He was a physician.

The symptoms of sickness are a fact. God's Word is truth. Truth takes authority over facts and changes them.

I've seen it happen countless times in my own life. I get into a situation where God's Word says one thing, but the facts that are staring me in the face say another.

How do we get those facts to change and line up with the truth of the Word?

Consider Jesus to be the High Priest of your confession, the One given full responsibility and all the resources of heaven to see that your words—His Word spoken out of your mouth—will come to pass in the earth. Consider Him!

Press toward the Target

Your *personal forecast*, or *confession of faith*, is never a personal boast, or a worried concern about the future. It's thankful and bold believing and receiving of God's promises in your life.

Sometimes we need to deal with the past in order to progress toward our God-given destiny. That's why one of the key foundations for this book is, *"Forgetting those things which are behind and reaching forward to those things which are ahead, I press toward the goal for the prize of the upward call of God in Christ Jesus,"* (Philippians 3:13-14).

You might be thinking: *Why would God want to bless my future? Why should I reach for the best I can be in Christ?*

God wants to bless you abundantly to establish His covenant (promises and divine plan) in the earth. God wants you to have a blessed life so you can help others realize their destiny in Christ, help the poor and suffering, and encourage others in godly living. (See Psalm 35:27.)

God has granted to us a phenomenal power in our words. We can speak great blessing and healing for our lives—and the lives of everyone we meet.

Words are spiritual. Words are powerful!

Don't just report on the past, or what you have and see today—pray, talk about, and *forecast* what you need from God's Word for today and tomorrow.

You might be thinking, *if words are so important, I will have to be perfect in everything I say!*

Jesus is the only one who is perfect. Our challenge is to diligently follow Him and learn the lessons He taught.

Being imperfect is something I know a lot about. But I also know where the target is.

It's right below your nose.

CPSIA information can be obtained at www.ICGtesting.com
Printed in the USA
LVOW12s0004021213

363458LV00015B/572/P

9 781628 713398